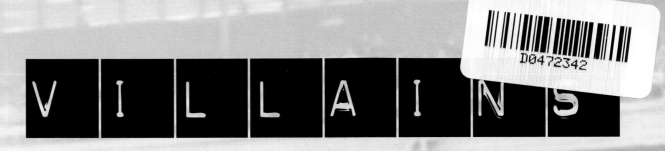

VILLAINS

THE BAD BOYS AND GIRLS OF SPORTS

KEN RAPPOPORT AND BARRY WILNER

For my father, who made all of our lives more colorful.

Thanks, Dad. —K.R.

To Helene, Nicole, Jamie, Tricia and Evan for their love,

support, and total lack of villainy. —B.W.

VILLAINS

The Bad Boys and Girls of Sports

by Ken Rappoport and Barry Wilner

© 2000 Design and compilation Lionheart Books, Ltd.

All rights reserved. Printed in Canada. No part of this book may be used

or reproduced in any manner whatsoever without written permission except in the case of

reprints in the context of reviews. For information, write Stark Books, an Andrews McMeel

Publishing imprint, 4520 Main Street, Kansas City, Missouri 64111.

Library of Congress Cataloging-in-Publication Data

Wilner, Barry.
  Villains: the bad boys and girls of sports/Barry Wilner and Ken Rappoport [i.e. Rappoport].
    p.cm
  ISBN: 0-7407-1218-7 (pbk.)
    1. Sports-Biography. 2. Scandals—History—20th Century. I. Rappoport, Ken II. Title.
GV697. A1 W543 2000
796'.092'2-dc21   00-58342
[B]

Design: Jill Dible

ATTENTION: SCHOOLS AND BUSINESSES

Andrews McMeel books are available at quantity discounts with bulk purchase for educational,

business, or sales promotional use. For information, please write to: Special Sales Department,

Andrews McMeel Publishing, 4520 Main Street, Kansas City, Missouri 64111.

Produced by Lionheart Books, Ltd.

Atlanta, Georgia 30341

TOP 25 VILLAINS

1 • Ty Cobb

2 • Mike Tyson

3 • Bob Knight

4 • Don King

5 • Ben Johnson

6 • Pete Rose

7 • John McEnroe

8 • Tonya Harding

9 • Marge Schott

10 • Jack Tatum

11 • George Steinbrenner

12 • Alan Eagleson

13 • Dave Schultz

14 • Avery Brundage

15 • Dennis Rodman

16 • Frank Kush

17 • Latrell Sprewell

18 • Woody Hayes

19 • Eddie Shore

20 • Ilie Nastase

21 • Denny McLain

22 • Billy Martin

23 • Tiger Williams

24 • Conrad Dobler

25 • Bill Laimbeer

TOP 5 VILLAINOUS TEAMS

1 • Chicago Black Sox

2 • Detroit Pistons' "Bad Boys"

3 • Philadelphia Flyers' "Broad Street Bullies"

INTRODUCTION

How do you define a sports villain? Well, some of them aren't villains in the true sense of the word, but, as far as most fans are concerned, they still wear black hats.

To Brooklyn Dodgers fans in 1951, there was no one more villainous than Bobby Thomson, who sent an entire borough into shock—and mourning—with a pennant-winning home run for the New York Giants. The Shot Heard 'Round the World was pure nirvana for Giants fans.

Dodgers fans were again dressed in black seven years later when Walter O'Malley moved the Bums to Los Angeles. West Coast baseball fans were thrilled to have the team.

And no one was more villainous to Utah Jazz fans than Michael Jordan after he snatched the 1998 NBA championship away from their team with his last-minute heroics for the Chicago Bulls. In Chicago, Jordan's legend was enhanced even more.

Though there's no question that these incidents affected fans deeply, even adversely, we decided to use a less subjective criteria when selecting the people to be profiled in this anthology. Based upon our experience as writers who have attended a wide variety of sporting events over the course of our careers, we believe sports villains to be athletes who have in some way betrayed the public trust, athletes who have, in short, blatantly ignored the rules of good sportsmanship and common decency. From trash-talking (Gary Payton) to tossing people into trash cans (Bob Knight), the people in this book are guilty of some kind of obnoxious and offensive behavior. In some cases, they have even been guilty of breaking the law.

To determine whether our selections are in accord with those of our colleagues, as well as to aid us in compiling a more objective, representative list of athletes who fall into the category of sports villain, we conducted an informal survey of more than forty experts in the area of professional sports, a diverse group of writers, broadcasters, executives, and coaches affiliated with such organizations as The Associated Press, *USA Today*, *Sports Illustrated*, *New York Times*, ESPN, Gannett and Copley news services, *Newsday*, *New York Daily News*, *Atlanta Constitution*, *Detroit Free Press*, the *National Post* in Canada, the U.S. Olympic Committee, NASCAR, Arena Football, radio station WFAN in New York, and the New York Sports Hall of Fame. It should be noted that any opinion expressed by these individuals does not represent the viewpoints or policies of the organization for whom they work.

The characters in *Villains* are, literally, bad news, all having made their share of negative headlines. Naturally, some have enjoyed the publicity and used it to promote their villainous behavior, such as Bill Laimbeer and Dennis Rodman of the Detroit Pistons and Dave Schultz of the Philadelphia Flyers.

Laimbeer, Rodman, and Schultz are among our list of "Top 25" all-time sports villains. So are Mike Tyson and Ty Cobb, for obvious reasons. And the Flyers are listed under our "Top 5" all-time villainous teams: if you went to a fight in the 1970s and a hockey game broke out, it was probably the "Broad Street Bullies" doing their thing.

And then there are Bob Knight, Woody Hayes, and Frank Kush, all of them hands-on coaches in the worst sense of the phrase. Of course, they all made most everyone's all-villains list, along with Pete Rose and the 1919 Chicago Black Sox, for their unethical behavior.

Owners George Steinbrenner, keeper of the infamous Bronx Zoo, and Marge Schott, who alienated players and fans alike in Cincinnati, are featured in the Top 25. So are John McEnroe and Ilie Nastase, who continually put their foot in their mouths, and Ben Johnson, who lost the respect of a once proud country after using drugs to attain victory.

Our fellow sports writers generally agreed with our Top 25 choices, although not everyone agreed on their ranking. "I think [Latrell] Sprewell is way too low [at No. 17] for what he did, a physical attack on a coach," said Jim Litke, sports columnist for The Associated Press. "[Bill] Laimbeer is slightly too low [No. 25]— he was a very nasty player. What did Frank Kush [No. 16] do to deserve being on this list?"

Said Mike Nadel, sports columnist for Copley news service:

"I know that it is difficult to really devise a 'system' to rank people for whom different criteria is used to judge one's 'villainousness.' For example, I can guarantee that Bob Knight fans—a very vocal group—aren't going to like him being placed that high [No. 3]. That's where I had him, too, though my top two were [Mike] Tyson and O.J. [Simpson].

"The only things that stick out on your list was the complete omission of O.J. and the ranking of [John] McEnroe so high [at No. 7]. Yes, I know that O.J. was found innocent in court, but both the civil trial and the court of public appeals

Referee Bill Oakes (21) separates Dennis Rodman and Alonzo Mourning (33) after Rodman was called for a second technical foul.

found him guilty of a fairly serious crime [if you can call your run-of-the-mill double homicide fairly serious]. As for McEnroe, yes, he had a temper and was a 'bad boy,' but the next several people on your list are complete villains. McEnroe a bigger villain than [Jack] Tatum, Schott, Steinbrenner or [Tonya] Harding? Hardly."

Roy McGregor, award-winning columnist for the *National Post* in Canada, named "the entire NBA" on his list of villains. We wouldn't go that far, but the NBA is well represented here with its disagreeable trend of trash-talking.

Make no mistake, the people in this book have been successful, many of them reaching the pinnacle of their profession at some point. Maybe this proves that Leo Durocher was right after all when he said, "Nice guys finish last."

Here, then, are their stories. See if you don't agree.

NASTY CHARACTERS

THE GEORGIA PEACH

They're great athletes with great enthusiasm and great devotion, not to mention disagreeable dispositions and a real mean streak.

Meet Ty Cobb in a competitive situation and he would beat you anyway he could. Literally. Say the same for Mike Tyson, whose bite is often worse than his bark.

And then there was Eddie Shore, who gave himself and hockey a bad name with his ferocious play on the ice. On the street, he would have been arrested for assault and battery.

So, read on—if you dare—and meet some of sport's masters of mayhem.

When Ty Cobb retired from baseball, he left a legacy of unmatched accomplishments, including twelve batting titles, a .367 career batting average, and 4,191 hits. He also left a legacy of grief.

With a mean streak and a monstrous temper to match, he was the most feared player of his time. Whether sliding into a base with his spikes high to tear apart the fielder or going into the stands to tear apart an abusive fan, Cobb was simply a terror during the twenty-three years he played from 1905 to 1928.

Woe to anyone who stood in his way, even the president of the United States! According to one story, Dwight Eisenhower was about to address the ball on a golf course when he heard a shrill, "Get the hell out of my way!" from down the fairway. Eisenhower turned to see a defiant Cobb, long since retired, charging up the green. The president stepped aside to let the ex-ballplayer go through. It's likely that the hell-raising Hall of Famer was the only one who could have pulled off such an audacious stunt.

What made Cobb so aggressive and mean? Some say it was an incident from his youth.

The story most told is that William Herschel Cobb, Ty's father, had left their Royston,

Although Ty Cobb left a legacy of impressive accomplishments when he retired from baseball, he was also known for his mean streak and a monstrous temper to match.

Georgia, home one August night in 1905, only to double back without anyone's knowledge. The elder Cobb, so the story goes, believed that his wife was cheating on him and hoped to catch her in the act.

Climbing onto the roof of his house, he attempted to enter his wife's bedroom through a window when a shotgun blast rang out. Amanda Cobb had pulled the trigger, mistaking her husband for a burglar. The blast killed William Cobb immediately. Amanda Cobb was acquitted at the subsequent trial, and the younger Cobb never had the satisfaction of performing before his beloved father on a major league baseball field.

"My father had his head blown off with a shotgun when I was eighteen years old," Cobb said later in life. "I didn't get over that. I've never gotten over that."

Cobb was playing minor league ball in Georgia at the time of his father's death, and with some self-promotion, was about to propel himself into the major leagues.

Sportswriting great Grantland Rice had received rave letters about an amazing young outfielder playing in the Sally League. As it turned out, Cobb had sent the letters himself without signing his name.

"I was in a hurry," Cobb said.

He came into the big-time full-throttle, with

flashing spikes and a huge chip on his shoulder. Accounts of his volcanic temper would fill volumes—battles under the bleachers with umpires, fights in alleyways with toughs, slugfests with players in hotel rooms. Cobb once beat up roommate Nap Rucker because Rucker had beaten Cobb to the bathtub following a game.

"I have to be first in everything," Cobb told Rucker.

Cobb was the guy fans and players loved to hate, and deservedly so. Whenever the Detroit Tigers traveled, Cobb was the team's No. 1 villain. Usually fans threw objects at him, mostly hard wads of paper. One time Cobb received

death threats after an infamous spiking incident against Philadelphia A's star "Home Run" Baker.

But it was an incident involving a fan that seemed to sum up Cobb's approach to life and baseball.

Early into the 1912 season, the Tigers were playing a game in New York. Fans were always hazing Cobb, but none with more venom than one man that day sitting twelve rows up. His name was Claude Lueker.

Lueker showed no mercy, calling Cobb every name in the book and then some. Anger rose slowly within Cobb until he could take it no longer. Finally, he jumped into the stands, climbed the rows to Lueker's seat, and administered a brutal beating to the heckler.

"He hit me in the face with his fist, knocked me down, jumped on me, kicked me, spiked me, and booted me in the ear," Lueker said later in his report to the police.

Cobb showed no remorse, despite the fact that he had just beaten up a man who had lost one hand in a printing press accident and had three fingers missing from the other. "I don't care if he didn't have any feet," said Cobb.

American League president Ban Johnson suspended Cobb, sparking a strike by his Detroit teammates. The Tigers weren't so much concerned about Cobb as they were about the protection of players from abusive fans. The strike lasted only one game, with a bunch of semi-pros filling in for the Tigers' regulars. And the crusty Cobb came back after twelve games, ready as usual to battle the world.

Spiking fielders was but one aspect of Cobb's game. His quick thinking and aggressive baserunning intimidated opponents, often forcing them to commit errors. Cobb sought to not only beat opponents but humiliate them.

IRON MIKE

. . . Mike Tyson has bitten Evander Holyfield for a second time and it is all-out war!

—Ringside announcers describing the action at the June 1997 championship fight between Mike Tyson and Evander Holyfield

In 1994, a survey group came out with statistics about athletes who have generated the greatest amount of negative news coverage.

The champ? Boxer Mike Tyson.

At the time the survey was conducted, 9,906 stories alone had been written about Tyson's troubles outside of the ring—too numerous to mention here.

Second was O.J. Simpson, who had merely faced double-murder charges. He wasn't even close. The former football player finished way behind Tyson at 6,754.

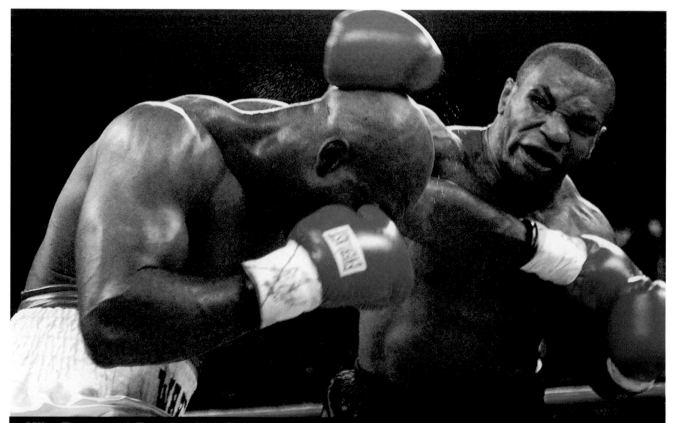

Mike Tyson and Evander Holyfield exchange punches during their WBA heavyweight match. The fight was stopped after Tyson bit off a piece of Holyfield's ear.

Rounding out the top ten: Ben Johnson, Pete Rose, Michael Jordan, Dwight Gooden, Tonya Harding, Charles Barkley, Darryl Strawberry, and Len Bias.

Johnson made news for using performance-enhancing drugs, Rose for gambling and tax evasion, Jordan for gambling, Gooden for substance abuse, Harding for allegedly conspiring to injure skating rival Nancy Kerrigan, Barkley for spitting on fans and throwing people through windows, Strawberry for substance abuse and Bias for a drug overdose that killed him.

As for Tyson's margin of "victory" over Simpson, imagine how much larger it would have been had the survey been carried through 1997, the year of the infamous "Bite of the Century"? That was only one of the

At age thirty-two, Tyson said he had experienced everything but death. "But," he added, "I think I've been to hell."

headlines to flash across America as newspapers had a field day with puns after Tyson bit off a piece of Evander Holyfield's ear during their second fight and then came back for more.

"Never let it be said Mike Tyson's bark is worse than his bite," one sports journalist wrote. "For Mike Tyson, the Old Testament credo of an eye for an eye and a tooth for a tooth wasn't enough," wrote another.

Biting an opponent was nothing new in boxing, of course. Fritzie Zivic, a Hall of Famer, was in the habit of biting opponents' ears when he fought in the 1930s and '40s. And heavyweight Andrew Golota, twice disqualified for low blows, also nibbled on an opponent's ear.

Looking back at the less than noble moment months later, Tyson was contrite. "I just totally lost it."

Along with losing his self-control, he lost $3 million, the fine levied against him for the outrageous incident. Tyson was initially banned from boxing by the Nevada Athletic Commission, but the ban was lifted after nineteen months. He made his comeback with a victory over Francois Botha in 1999. Tyson was still a big draw, a compelling name. But by then he had lost much of the luster he had gained as the two-time world heavyweight champion.

At one time, Tyson was considered just about indestructible—by everyone, that is, except Buster Douglas, who pulled off a stunning upset in Japan. Tyson, a 50–1 favorite in that 1990 fight, was blamed for underestimating his opponent. It never happened again, although Iron Mike went through a meltdown period after spending four years in prison once he was convicted of raping a beauty pageant contestant in Indianapolis.

As he charged through life like the proverbial bull in a china shop, Tyson was a news story waiting to happen. Every day there seemed to be something new on the docket—divorce proceedings, lawsuits (including a raging battle with promoter Don King over earnings), tax problems and any number of sordid incidents. Tyson not only landed in court time and again but also back in jail when he violated parole with a scuffle following a fender-bender on the road.

Since leaving the Catskills some twenty years ago under the nurturing of trainer Cus D'Amato, Tyson had traveled a rocky road. At age thirty-two, he said, he had experienced everything but death. "But," he added, "I think I've been to hell."

"Never let it be said Mike Tyson's bark is worse than his bite," one journalist wrote about the WBA heavyweight match held on June 28, 1997 in which Evander Holyfield lost a piece of his ear but retained his title. Tyson lost his self-control and was banned from boxing for nineteen months.

HATEFUL HITS

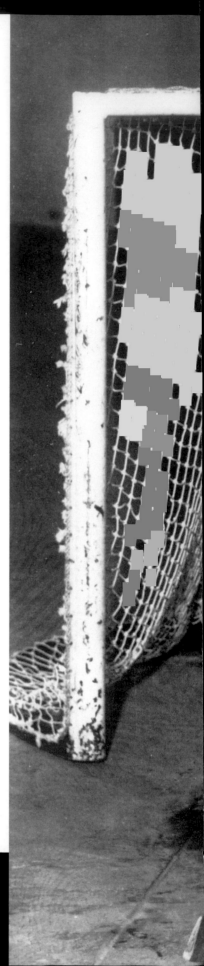

Hockey isn't for the fainthearted, but no player has yet been killed in the NHL by a hard check or a cheap shot. Yet it almost occurred during the 1933–1934 season.

Ace Bailey, meet Eddie Shore.

On the night of December 12, 1933, they did, indeed, meet—in a collision that very nearly cost Bailey his life. Newspapers had already set up obituary stories for Irvin "Ace" Bailey after the Toronto left winger suffered severe head injuries in the ghastly collision with the bellicose Boston defenseman.

Shore had a well-deserved reputation as a tough player. But after the crack-up with Bailey, he also gained a reputation as a *dirty* player.

Shore was carrying the puck out of his own zone on a Boston power play when Toronto defenseman Red Horner knocked him down with a hip-check. Horner passed the puck over to defenseman King Clancy, who initiated a counterattack.

Bailey dropped back to take Clancy's place on defense and Shore, blind with fury over being dumped into the corner, was looking for someone to hit back. He headed for Bailey, who had his back to Shore and was completely oblivious to the hard-charging defenseman.

"What I always believed is that Shore thought he was attacking me," Horner said. "He wanted to get even for the check I had just put on him. He thought Bailey was me."

Shore's surprise—and savage—attack flipped Bailey over backward, sending him crashing to the ice on his head. There he lay like a man breathing his last, his legs twitching.

Furious at the attack, Horner went after Shore with a vengeance and knocked him unconscious. Shore lay on the ice, blood gushing from his head.

Both injured players were rushed to the hospital, where surgeons removed a blood clot from Bailey's brain. The operation saved his life, but not his career. Shore, meanwhile, lived to play another day.

In an effort to raise money for Bailey, the Maple Leafs played an exhibition game against a team composed of the NHL's top players. It was the beginning of a tradition—the All-Star Game.

Both Bailey and Shore lived to ripe old ages: Shore died in 1985 at the age of eighty-two and Bailey in 1992 at eighty-eight.

Always known as a tough player, Eddie Shore once attacked an opponent so viciously that he flipped over backwards and crashed to the ice on his head. Surgeons were successful in removing a blood clot from his brain, but Ace Bailey never played hockey again. "That's all right, Eddie," Bailey said. "It's all part of the game."

TIGER WILLIAMS

During his fourteen seasons in the NHL, Tiger Williams was one of the most feared players in the league. Not for his scoring, but for his stickwork.

Even opposing coaches weren't safe from Williams' rapier-like hockey stick. Scotty Bowman once made the mistake of leaning too far over the sideboards to watch a fight in progress and went crashing to the floor with a bad head wound.

"His head was in the wrong place at the wrong time," Williams said, recalling the incident. "Scotty Bowman's job is to coach, and a coach is supposed to stay behind the bench. But his head was sticking out, watching a fight. I just happened to skate by the Buffalo bench and my stick must have accidentally touched him."

While his victims usually wound up on their backs or face down on the ice, Williams almost always wound up in the penalty box—and eventually in the office of Brian O'Neill, who at the time dispensed discipline for the NHL. Season after season, while playing in Toronto, Vancouver, Detroit, Los Angeles and Hartford, Williams was usually among the league leaders in penalty minutes—and suspensions.

Not that he would ever admit his guilt.

"Somehow, players grab me and my stick and put it in their own face," Williams once said, tongue in cheek.

Statistics alone do not tell the story of the intimidation factor Williams presented on the ice, but his numbers are indeed formidable. Twelve years after retiring in 1988, Williams is still the NHL's all-time leader in penalty minutes with 3,966, an average of 4.12 a game. Heading into the 1999–2000 season, that was 401 minutes more than runner-up Dale Hunter, who played five more seasons and in 445 more games.

Combined with 455 penalty minutes in the playoffs, Williams' grand total of 4,421 PIMs added up to more than seventy entire regular-season games of sitting in the penalty box.

At the time that Williams was traded to Los Angeles from Detroit in the 1984–85 season, Kings star Dave Taylor seemed relieved he wouldn't have to face him on the ice. "He knows how to bother you," Taylor said of Williams. "He's always hooking you, grabbing you, rubbing a glove in your face."

Dave Williams was a terror even while growing up on the prairies of Western Canada. He acquired the nickname of "Tiger" early in life, so the story goes, while playing in a youth hockey game. Unhappy with a ruling made by the referee, he simply punched him. It didn't matter to Williams that the referee was his older brother.

It was the first of many punches thrown by Williams in a stormy hockey career that featured some of the wildest brawls and most notorious stick fights in NHL history. Tiger once faced assault charges after hitting Pittsburgh's Dennis Owchar over the head with his stick. He also engaged Los Angeles' Dave Hutchinson in a vicious stick duel during the playoffs, and—just imagine—the battle occurred while both were in the penalty box! And Williams wasn't above going into the stands, either, once charging after a fan at the LA Forum after he had thrown ice at Williams.

Williams never showed much remorse for his villainous behavior. It was, after all, part of his job description. When his team needed someone to start trouble, Williams was only too eager to do so.

"Fighting was just another tactic in the game," said Williams, who scored 241 goals in his career and probably would have doubled that if he didn't spend so much time sitting in the penalty box.

"It's like slowing the game down if a game isn't going the way you want it to. You try to alter the flow of the game by engaging in a fight with their so-called tough guy. It's an intimidating factor to give your team an edge."

SOME OF THE UGLIEST INCIDENTS

● Oakland Raiders linebacker **Jack Tatum** lived up to his nickname as "The Assassin" with a vicious tackle of New England receiver Darryl Stingley during an exhibition game with the Patriots on August 12, 1978. Stingley was left paralyzed, a quadraplegic.

● Ray Fosse's head may still be ringing from this violent encounter with **Pete Rose** during the 1970 All-Star Game. "Charlie Hustle" came home with the winning run for the National League with a forceful, frightening hit that loosened the ball from Fosse's hand and fractured his shoulder. The Cleveland catcher was never quite the same. Apparently, someone forgot to tell Rose that it was only an exhibition game.

● **Ulf Samuelsson** will forever be enshrined in the Boston Bruins' Hall of Shame, thanks to his nasty leg check of Cam Neely in the 1991 playoffs that hobbled the Bruins' top scorer. Samuelsson, playing for Pittsburgh, then finished his job on Neely a couple of days later with a violent hit that knocked him out of the playoffs and, soon, out of hockey.

● New York Islanders great **Denis Potvin** wasn't so great in the eyes of New York Rangers fans, particularly after knocking Ulf Nilsson out of the 1979 playoffs. In breaking Nilsson's ankle with a vicious, teeth-chattering hit, Potvin effectively ended the Rangers' run for the Stanley Cup. To this day, no Rangers game at Madison Square Garden is official without the crowd chanting, "Potvin sucks!"

IN SPORTS HISTORY

- **Dale Hunter** built a reputation as one of the nastiest—and dirtiest—players in hockey, a reputation that was justified when he belted New York Islanders forward Pierre Turgeon in the back with his stick. Hunter's misdeed occurred as Turgeon was skating away after scoring a goal against Washington in the 1993 NHL playoffs. The blow knocked Turgeon out of the playoffs while Hunter received a twenty-game suspension that carried into the following season.

- **Wayne Maki** and **Marty McSorley**, players from different eras, also fit into the category of "Hateful Hitmen" because of their stick work. In 1969, Wayne Maki's blow to the head of "Terrible" Ted Green forced him to miss a season. Green returned to hockey with a steel plate in his head. McSorley's premeditated blow from behind left Donald Brashear with a concussion. McSorley was suspended for twenty-three games—the remainder of the 1999–2000 season.

- One of the most violent brawls in college basketball history occurred during the Ohio State-Minnesota game on January 25, 1972. The "basketbrawl" sent Ohio State's Luke Witte and teammate Mark Wagar to the hospital and resulted in the suspensions of Minnesota's **Corky Taylor** and **Ron Behagen**. Militaristic Minnesota coach Bill Musselman was largely criticized for his team's aggressive behavior.

- **Chuck Bednarik** was the last of football's sixty-minute men, but he'll also be remembered for his famous hit on Frank Gifford in a game between the Philadelphia Eagles and New York Giants in 1960. The Giants' back had just caught a pass and taken a couple of steps when Bednarik, in his own words, "waffled him." Gifford's head snapped back and, for a moment, it looked like it had been separated from his shoulders. Fortunately, only the ball went rolling away. Gifford had been knocked unconscious.

- When the Houston Rockets' Rudy Tomjanovich was helped off the court after a savage beating by **Kermit Washington** on December 9, 1977, he knew he had really been hurt. He just didn't know how badly. A fractured skull, broken jaw, broken nose, and leakage of spinal fluid were only some of the injuries that Tomjanovich suffered at the hands of the enraged Los Angeles Lakers forward during a brawl that involved several players. Washington was fined $10,000 and suspended for sixty days.

NASTY COACHES AND MANAGERS

A DARK AND STORMY KNIGHT

Bob Knight is a throwback, they say. That's what some people at Indiana University would like to do to him after his latest embarrassing episode —throw him back.

But after three stormy decades at the Big Ten school, Knight has somehow established a beachhead against his critics, ducked the slings and arrows of outraged alumni, and remained untouchable as the Hoosiers' basketball coach.

Not so fortunate were Woody Hayes at Ohio State and Frank Kush at Arizona State, who were notorious for their abusive tactics while coaching football. Both were fired.

Here they are along with other coaches and managers who have, perhaps, taken the game a bit too seriously.

Punch a cop. Attack a player. Clout a coach. Bob Knight is liberal-minded when it comes to assault and battery, an equal opportunity aggressor. And these are but a few of the notorious episodes in the ongoing soap opera featuring Indiana University's fiery basketball coach.

Knight's heroes include George and Woody. No, not George Carlin and Woody Allen— General George S. Patton and Woody Hayes, the Ohio State football coach.

Like Patton, Knight has a militaristic approach to basketball. The Hoosiers approach every game as if they were going into battle. And for Knight many times it is a battle—quite literally.

Like Hayes, Knight does not take losing easily: he has attacked players, though never like the time Hayes slugged a Clemson player after his interception sealed Ohio State's fate in the 1979 Gator Bowl. But Knight has definitely been a hands-on coach.

Throwing water, throwing punches, throwing chairs on the court. Bob Knight was once described as "a cross between Simon Legree and Father Flanagan."

A little mayhem, yes. Murder, no.

"Maybe I've forgotten this, but I don't think I've ever shot anybody," said Knight.

Actually, Knight did nail a buddy with buckshot during a hunting expedition. It was an accident, of course. Then there was the time he fired a starter pistol at a sportswriter. No accident, just having a little fun. You *know* what he thinks about sportswriters.

Knight's confrontations with the press have been as numerous as his battles with just about everyone else. Once, when an out-of-town magazine writer talked to a player without Knight's permission, the coach shouted obscenities at him, threatened him, and kicked him out. Suffice to say, Knight has drawn more than his share of negative reaction from the media. Said one writer:

"Calling Bob Knight 'Bobby' is like calling George Patton 'Georgie.' It doesn't fit. Bob is the meanest sumbitch on two wheels. And remember, under that surface veneer of meanness lies a really thick layer of more meanness."

Not that Knight is all bad. He sprinkles occasional acts of kindness between his acts of rage. He can be as loyal to a friend as he is brutal to an enemy. He can be as different as, well, black and white.

Knight's positive impact can be found at many schools around the country, where his former players and assistants are coaching successfully. Many of them are Knight's disciples. But while he has generated ferocious support from his friends, he has sparked just as fierce opposition from his critics. Former Louisiana State coach Dale Brown once described Knight as "a despicable human being."

Others who have felt Knight's wrath would gladly second the motion. "He'll get away with the bullying and vulgarity only so long as he wins," said one midwestern basketball coach of Knight, an intelligent, literate man and passionate reader who seems to enjoy shocking people with his use of profanity.

Former Kentucky coach Joe Hall certainly is no fan of Bobby Knight. Once, during a game against Indiana, the Hoosiers were winning by a big score when Knight got up to berate an official.

"Way to go, Bobby," Hall yelled.

The two coaches were soon at the scorer's table exchanging words. Knight suddenly struck Hall on the side of the head. Knight would later say it was only "a playful tap." Hall didn't think so.

"He personally humiliated me," Hall said, "and I'll never forget it."

However, there are almost as many coaches who admire Knight as those that hate him. One of them is Northwestern's Kevin O'Neill, who nearly came to blows with Knight on the court one time but nevertheless respects him.

"He may not be Mr. Cuddles all the time," O'Neill said, "but in the long run what he could do for a kid would far outweigh the negatives."

If nothing else, Knight runs a clean program at Indiana. An unusually high percentage of his players graduate, which can't be said at many universities with such a high-profile basketball program. If he hasn't won much lately, he has won often enough—three national championships and eleven Big Ten titles—and coached the U.S. Olympic team to a gold medal at the 1984 Games. From Army to Indiana, he has fashioned rugged, uncompromising teams, an extension of his personality. To a certain extent, he re-invented the game. And he will go down as one of the greatest basketball coaches ever, but also one who was criticized for his lack of sensitivity and his shoot-from-the-mouth approach.

While charging to the top of his profession, Knight has left a path of destruction in his wake equaled by few coaches, college or pro.

Knight's teams at Army, like all the military academies, had height restrictions. That didn't stop him from turning out competitive teams that played brutally tough defense against the country's elite. Even in beating the Cadets, teams knew they had been in battle. Knight,

One of the greatest basketball coaches ever, Knight has also been criticized for his lack of sensitivity and his shoot-from-the-mouth approach.

who played on a national championship team at Ohio State, was both martinet and father confessor to the well-trained Cadets. He once was described as a "a cross between Simon Legree and Father Flanagan."

At Indiana, it was joked that Knight only promised his players hair shirts and indentured servitude—and a chance to play for the national championship year in and year out. The last part was no joke early in Knight's career. A fearful legend was born along the way.

Players and coaches haven't been the only victims of Knight's physical abuse. He sparked more national outrage when he threw a chair on the court to protest a referee's decision. And then he set off an international incident when he was arrested for assault and battery against a police officer while in Puerto Rico coaching the U.S. team at the 1979 Pan American Games. Knight, who punched the cop when he refused to remove a noisy Brazilian women's team from the gym during the U.S. team's practice session, was eventually convicted in absentia and sentenced to six months in prison. It must have been another proud moment for Knight when, on the team flight out of Puerto Rico, he pulled his pants down and exposed his derrière through a window. Some thought Knight was showing his best side.

Knight's lack of composure was almost comical—to everyone but the players who endured his wrath. One of the most celebrated incidents came early in Knight's career at Indiana in 1976, when, furious with the play of reserve guard Jim Wisman, he grabbed him by the shirt and hauled him off the court. The picture of the attack, featured in newspapers across the country, sparked a backlash of outrage. But no more than another incident eighteen years later when Knight butted his forehead against freshman Sherrod Wilkerson. This time, Knight's display was witnessed by a national television audience.

And then there was guard Neil Reed, who

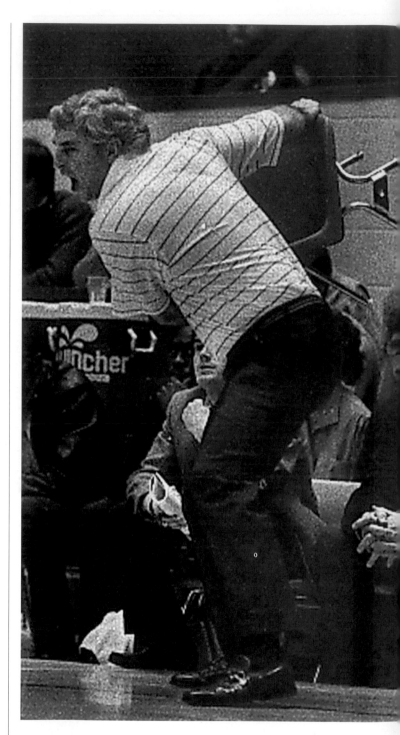

talked publicly of Knight's "verbal attacks and physical assaults." In one incident during a game against Ohio State, newspapers published a picture of Knight, his face twisted in rage, scolding Reed with his hands wrapped around the player's head.

The incident involving Reed put Knight in the most glaring spotlight of his career when it sparked an investigation by the school's trustees

Bob Knight winds up and throws a chair across the floor during Indiana's 72-63 loss to Purdue during the 1984–85 season.

that turned up other incidents of abuse. On May 15, 2000, Knight was suspended for three games in the 2000–2001 season, fined $30,000, and ordered to apologize to an athletic department secretary whom he berated and threatened on two occasions. Knight is also subject to a "zero-tolerance policy" in the future. University president Myles Brand stated that any further displays of misconduct by Knight deemed embarrassing to the school would result in his immediate dismissal. Knight's continuous "pattern of inappropriate behavior . . . cannot and will not be tolerated," said Brand.

Says one Knight friend:

"I told Bob a long time ago, if you're going to alienate so many people, then you better win and win big. Because when you don't, they're going to be lined up to shoot you down when you fail."

OTHER TEMPERAMENTAL TYPES

Bob Knight isn't the only coach whose temper tantrums get him into frequent trouble. Here are some other manhandlers who had similar problems:

Ohio State football coach Woody Hayes didn't stop at abusing players. He once attacked a cameraman who was recording his reaction to losing a game.

• **WOODY HAYES.** Like Knight, the Ohio State football coach was a bad loser known for a physical style of coaching. He didn't stop there. Hayes also went after players on the other team, not to mention a cameraman.

Enraged after a fumble ended any hope of a comeback against Michigan in 1977, Hayes attacked ABC-TV cameraman Mike Freedman. The cameraman was standing five yards away recording Hayes' reaction to the impending loss.

However, that wasn't the pièce de résistance of Hayes' successful but troubled career. At the 1979 Gator Bowl, Hayes attacked Clemson middle guard Charlie Bauman, who had intercepted a pass that sealed the Buckeyes' 17-15 loss. Hayes lost more than the game—he lost his job over the incident.

One bystander joked that Hayes went after the wrong man. "I think Woody ought to have hit Art Schlichter. He's the one who threw the pass."

• **FRANK KUSH.** After a tumultuous football coaching career, Kush found work running a reform school in Arizona. To Kevin Rutledge, it suited him. No one—particularly Rutledge—would have expected Kush to end up teaching a course at Dale Carnegie.

Kush was fired as coach of Arizona State in 1979 in the wake of a lawsuit filed by Rutledge, a Sun Devils punter who charged that the coach punched him in the face during a 1978 game against Washington. Luckily for Kush, the court case was held in Maricopa County, where he was simply a local god.

The trial ended in Kush's favor with a hung jury, but he was dismissed by Arizona State for allegedly persuading staff members to change their stories about the incident. In the wake of Kush's firing, Arizona State went on NCAA probation that prohibited television appearances and bowl games for two years.

It wasn't exactly Comfort Farm for Arizona State football players during Kush's regime of terror for twenty-one-plus years. Among the horrors at Kush's Marine-like training camps: "Mt. Kush," an 800-foot climb for insubordinate players. Over the years, Kush eventually regained some dignity when the playing surface at Sun Devils Stadium was renamed "Frank Kush Field" in 1996.

"It's like naming a stadium after O.J. Simpson," Rutledge said.

• **LEO DUROCHER.** Whether kicking dirt on umpires or cursing players and reporters, Durocher was one of baseball's angriest managers for thirty-two years from 1941–1973.

Durocher coined the expression, "Nice guys finish last," and he lived it to the letter. Nicknamed "Leo the

Lip," Durocher never sought to win any popularity contests. But he did win plenty of games (2,008), three pennants, and one World Series during his career.

Unfortunately, Durocher will be remembered as much for his one-year suspension from baseball in 1947 when he was manager of the Brooklyn Dodgers. Commissioner Happy Chandler banned Durocher for his relationship with "unsavory" characters.

● **MIKE KEENAN.** He has been immediately successful just about everywhere he has coached in the NHL—and he has just as quickly worn out his welcome.

With his abrasive, all-or-nothing style, Keenan seems to have the right touch for a quick fix. Over the long haul, though, his approach rubs his players—and others—the wrong way.

After firing Keenan in Philadelphia, Flyers general manager Bobby Clarke said: "He was very demanding of the players, which I think is necessary. But I thought in Philly he went overboard. He was abusive to the players. He was verbally abusive to them and he degraded some of them."

Only once did Keenan make an exit of his own choosing—after leading the New York Rangers to the Stanley Cup in 1994. His departure after only one year took everyone by surprise because he still had four more years left on his contract. But Keenan took advantage of a loophole in his contract to escape, leaving a bitter taste for club officials and fans alike.

"Nice guys finish last" was an expression coined by Leo "The Lip" Durocher. And he proved it by winning 2,008 games, three pennants, and one World Series.

Keenan wound up in St. Louis, where he eventually coached Wayne Gretzky. Then he alienated the greatest player in hockey history, who left the Blues as a free agent—for Keenan's former team, the Rangers.

● **BILLY MARTIN.** The mercurial Martin, with his two-fisted approach, very well could be regarded as a latter-day Durocher. A noted brawler, he created as many headlines off the field as he did on it.

Martin managed from 1969–1988, setting the tone of his managerial career in his first year at Minnesota with an altercation involving pitcher Dave Boswell. He was fired by the Twins that season after leading the team to the AL West championship.

Martin was, of course, known mostly for his association with the New York Yankees as a feisty player and manager. His explosive, symbiotic relationship with George Steinbrenner reached almost comical, soap-opera proportions: Martin was hired and fired five times by the Yankees owner.

Tossed from the game for arguing balls and strikes, Martin responds by kicking dirt on home plate umpire Dallas Parks.

RENEGADE RAIDERS

You don't have to be mean-spirited to win championships—but it doesn't hurt, as was the case with the Oakland Raiders, Detroit Pistons, Philadelphia Flyers, and Boston Bruins. At one time or another, those teams were short on patience, long on intimidation.

The Raiders flourished longer than any of them, winning an NFL championship in the '70s and then two more in the '80s with a hell-raising team second to none.

Of course, Philadelphia's rugged "Broad Street Bullies" and Boston's boisterous "Big Bad Bruins" would just as soon beat you in the alley as beat you on the ice. And Detroit's "Bad Boys"? They just beat you up.

They weren't exactly the kind of people you would want to meet in a dark alley or on a football field. Just imagine running into these characters: The Assassin and Kick 'Em in the Head Ted (alias "The Mad Stork").

No, they weren't characters from *The Godfather*. They were the rough and ready group that wore Raiders uniforms for many years, both in Oakland and Los Angeles. It was in Oakland in the '60s and '70s when the Raiders established a well-earned reputation as troublemakers.

Oakland, California: Home of the Hell's

Angels, the Black Panthers, and the Raiders. That was Ben Davidson's joke. "It was that kind of a city and that kind of a team," he said.

About the same time, Boston's "Big, Bad Bruins" and then the Philadelphia Flyers' "Broad Street Bullies" were wreaking havoc in hockey. Later, it was the Detroit Pistons' "Bad Boys" in basketball.

Four teams, three sports, one style. Few teams in American sports history matched that Fearsome Foursome for villainous behavior.

"We all knew when something had to happen,

Ben Davidson had a reputation as one of the dirtiest players in the game. He once made a late hit on Joe Namath that broke the quarterback's jaw.

Los Angeles Raiders general managing partner Al Davis (left) helped to forge the tough image of the Raiders when they were in Oakland. He decided to make black the more dominant color of the uniform because he thought it looked more ominous.

and if there was a chance to do something to turn it around, then we did it," said Davidson.

In his time, Davidson had a reputation as one of the dirtiest players in the game. Note his late hit that broke Joe Namath's jaw.

And beware the receiver that crossed into the territory of Raiders safety Jack "The Assassin" Tatum and linebacker Ted "Mad Stork" Hendricks. Or George Atkinson.

The Raiders were a collection of renegades, rebels, and reclamation projects in a league that didn't look kindly on flamboyance. In an NFL that was clean-cut and conservative, the Raiders assumed the role of the anti-establishment. The Raiders broke the mold, wearing mustaches,

beards, and goatees. No ties and jackets required. All they did was win and rub your nose in it.

"We had to be the hairiest group in the NFL," said John Vella, who played on the offensive line. "I played in Minnesota one year, and that group looked like choirboys after coming from the Raiders."

The guiding hand of the Raiders was Al Davis, who was called a Machiavellian figure by some and a "genius" by others. If he had a genius for anything, it was picking players off the scrap heap and making champions out of them. Under Davis, the Raiders were the only team to reach the Super Bowl in the '60s, '70s and '80s. The Raiders won the NFL's big prize three times—once after the team had moved to Los Angeles.

It only took Davis fourteen years in LA to see that he had made a mistake. It was back to Oakland in the '90s in one of the most bizarre team relocation stories in sports history.

One of Davis' first moves when he came to Oakland in 1963 was to make black a more dominant color in the Raiders' uniforms. He thought it would give his team a psychological edge because it looked more ominous. To many, the Raiders' logo expressed their philosophy as much as anything—the drawing of a helmeted player wearing an eye patch with a background of crossed swords. Not exactly Mr. Nice Guy. All that was missing was a dagger between his teeth.

Football was a game that was supposed to be fun. But one look at that logo and you knew that playing the Raiders was going to be rough. Walking the plank sounded better than walking onto the field to meet this pugnacious group.

Nor, for that matter, did the Raiders save their nastiness for game day. During one practice, Hendricks kicked fullback Marv Hubbard in the head while Hubbard was on the ground. Thus was born "Kick 'Em in the Head, Ted." (Never mind that Hubbard just happened to be Hendricks' roommate.)

Hendricks was one of the wildest characters on those hell-for-leather Raiders teams. He came to Oakland as a free agent in 1975 after his promising career appeared to have blown up. A star at the University of Miami, Hendricks was drafted as a linebacker by the Baltimore Colts and dubbed "The Mad Stork" because of his six foot seven height, long neck, and off-the-wall demeanor.

Hendricks became a premier player in Baltimore, but also a premier pain in the neck—literally. Talented but troubled, Hendricks had developed a reputation as a player who tackled high and with his forearm. In the football vernac-

ular, *clotheslining*. It was easy to break someone's neck that way. It was a tactic not condoned anywhere in football and particularly not in Baltimore, where Don Shula ran a straight and narrow ship. Hendricks also drank as hard as he played. He was eventually traded to Green Bay, where he lasted just one season. He later signed with the World Football League's Jacksonville Sharks, but they folded without playing a game. Who would take on Hendricks, who was generally regarded as a troublemaker, misfit, and dirty player?

Welcome to Oakland, Ted.

Fellow linebacker and friend Phil Villapiano remembered that "everything 'Kick 'Em' did was weird."

A typical Hendricks story:

Raiders coach John Madden started every practice with the command, "Okay, let's get started." After two preseason losses, the practices were becoming longer and much too arduous to suit Hendricks' taste. Borrowing a friend's horse, Hendricks raced onto the practice field in full uniform and shouted, "Coach, let's get started!" Madden eased off after that.

Hendricks, who had won a Super Bowl ring in Baltimore, helped the Raiders win three—in 1976, 1980, and 1983. At the end of his career, Hendricks' drinking had become a problem not only for himself but for the team. In 1983 he attacked quarterback Marc Wilson in a bar. Recalls Raiders trainer George Anderson: "Ted always used to be a happy drunk. But at the end, he was getting a little mean."

"Mean" was a word usually attached to Ben Davidson, a six foot seven, 265-pound defensive end. Davidson had had problems with other teams, but he found a place in Oakland. He is best remembered for one incident against the Raiders' arch-rival Kansas City Chiefs in 1970. The Chiefs were leading 17-14 late in the game when Kansas City quarterback Len Dawson bootlegged the ball nineteen yards around the right end, deep into Oakland territory. With Dawson crouching on the ground, Davidson jumped on him. "Maybe it wasn't a very nice thing to do, but I honestly wasn't sure if Dawson was down or not," Davidson said in defending himself later.

Davidson's action sparked a melee that lasted some ten minutes and sparked the Raiders as well. They recovered to tie the game 17-17 on George Blanda's forty-eight-yard field goal with three seconds remaining. Looking back on the incident, Davidson was hardly remorseful. He felt that the play took the spirit out of the Chiefs and helped the Raiders win the division title. "The play was worth $18,000 a man, since we made the playoffs, so you could say it was cost-efficient."

The most notorious hit in Raiders history, though, was courtesy of Jack Tatum, a universally feared safety. The Raiders were playing the New England Patriots in an exhibition game on August 12, 1978. Darryl Stingley was running a slant pattern when Tatum viciously tackled the receiver in the neck. The collision dropped Stingley to the ground as if he had been shot. He lay motionless on the field as solemn players gathered around, including Tatum. "You expect him to jump up," Tatum once recalled. "I was hoping he just had the wind knocked out of him."

No such luck. Stingley was left paralyzed—a quadraplegic. A seemingly unremorseful Tatum later detailed that vicious hit, and many others, in a best-selling autobiography, *They Call Me Assassin*.

The incident heightened the image of the Raiders as a nasty team. It was rare when they weren't booed upon entering an opponent's stadium. But they were a team that thoroughly enjoyed playing the part of villains.

New England Patriots wide receiver Darryl Stingley lies motionless on the field after a vicious tackle by the Raiders' Jack Tatum. The injury left Stingley a quadraplegic.

DETROIT PISTONS' "BAD BOYS"

To know them was to hate them. They were good, but they were bad. Very, very bad. While bullying their way to the top of the NBA in 1989 and 1990, the Detroit Pistons might have been the most hated team in basketball history.

Make that sports history.

Actually, it was a love-hate relationship. Loved by their fans, hated by the opposition. Well, perhaps *hate* was too mild a word.

"You hate the Internal Revenue Service," Pistons trainer Mike Abdenour once said. "Take it a step further and you have what people feel for us."

Bill Laimbeer exemplified the play of the notorious "Bad Boys."

"I have a competitive nature," he said. "I did anything I could to win, and I came off as a mean, nasty guy." Pistons players, proud of their consecutive rough-and-tumble championships, called themselves hard-nosed. Opponents called them hard-headed, and that wasn't the only thing they called them.

Facing the Pistons in the 1991 playoffs, the Chicago Bulls' Michael Jordan saw the match-up as much more than just two teams fighting to win the NBA championship. To Jordan, it was a battle of philosophies: good vs. evil. If the Pistons won, other teams would try to copy their style and "that's not good for the game," Jordan said.

Jordan was justified in his assessment, particularly after Detroit's Dennis Rodman shoved Scottie Pippen head-first into the seats. On the street, Rodman might have been led away in handcuffs to face an assault charge.

In an earlier playoff series against the Bulls, Laimbeer was charged with three technical fouls in the first two games. He was kicked out of one game after his second elbowing incident. Just seconds before he was ejected, Laimbeer gave Pippen a two-handed shove after the referee had stopped play.

The Pistons' aggressive style was self-destructive in some ways. Coach Chuck Daly thought officials looked at his team "with a magnifying glass" because of its reputation. The players agreed. "Laimbeer gets blamed for everything," said Rodman.

Case in point: In the 1988 finals against Los Angeles, Laimbeer was called for a foul against Kareem Abdul-Jabbar. To some minds, it was a phantom foul. Nevertheless, Abdul-Jabbar went to the line to cash in free throws that denied the Pistons their first NBA title.

If there was some question about Laimbeer's foul against Abdul-Jabbar, there was no arguing his blatant attack on another superstar, Larry Bird. Millions saw it in a nationally televised playoff game. Bird didn't see it until it was too late. He was on the floor, looking up—the victim of a Laimbeer body slam.

The Pistons didn't mind their reputation for hard, physical play. Just about every member of the Pistons' organization reveled in the "Bad Boys" reputation—all the way up to general manager Jack McCloskey, who put together the menacing team.

"If I ever get to the pearly gates and St. Peter asks me, 'Who are you?' I'm going to say, 'I'm a Piston Bad Boy.'"

For two straight years, the Pistons pushed and pulled, clawed and battled their way to the NBA championship. Like a gang of villains in a Hollywood western, they rode into town and wiped out everything in sight. Even when they lost, they left their marks on the locals.

Dennis Rodman of the Detroit Pistons tries to snatch the ball away from falling New York Knicks forward Kiki Vandeweghe during a playoff game in Madison Square Garden.

Along with Laimbeer, Rodman and Rick Mahorn also shared top billing as leaders of the "Bad Boys."

Laimbeer was a ponderous six foot ten center who came out of Notre Dame with a reputation as a solid defensive player. McCloskey saw more than that in Laimbeer—he saw an *attitude*. Which is why he acquired him in a trade with Cleveland in 1982.

He was a big piece of the puzzle as the Pistons slowly built themselves into a contender in the '80s. It started with the selection of Isiah Thomas in the 1981 draft and continued with trades for Vinnie Johnson and Laimbeer. Johnson would earn the nickname "Microwave" for burning opponents off the bench as one of the league's top sixth men.

Then McCloskey made his key move, hiring Daly as coach in 1983. Daly had been fired by the Cleveland Cavaliers the season before after forty-one games. What did McCloskey see in Daly? A disposition that would shape the Pistons. "Don't trust happiness," was one of Daly's daily aphorisms. Another of his famous sayings: "No easy baskets!" Over-the-edge defense would eventually be the hallmark of the Pistons' success.

Mahorn, Joe Dumars, John Salley, and Rodman came later to help the Pistons make their assault on the title. Dumars was considered one of the few "Mr. Nice Guys" in the group. He also was the surest shot.

McCloskey was shocked to find that Dumars was still available when the Pistons' eighteenth pick came around in the 1985 draft. "I didn't have any hope that he would be there." But it seemed that Dumars was destined to be a Piston, same as Rodman. Because of poor performances in pre-draft tournaments and other workouts, Rodman's stock had dropped sharply for many NBA teams. But not for the Pistons, who took the product of little known Southeast Oklahoma State in the second round.

McCloskey had a hunch that Rodman could perform much better. As it turned out, an asthmatic condition had prevented Rodman from doing well at some camps. But, oh, could the kid rebound! McCloskey's faith was justified when Rodman became the No. 1 rebounder—and No. 1 renegade—in the NBA.

The Boston Celtics and Los Angeles Lakers had all but dominated the NBA in the '80s. Late in the decade, the Pistons decided it was their turn. They were not about to turn the other cheek.

"When the Pistons came into a town, all the media would write about were 'The Bad Boys' and how rough we played," Laimbeer said. "They'd be asking players if they were going to stand up to us. And once we got teams thinking like that, we had them. We already got them out of their game."

The Pistons paid for their indiscretions—to the tune of $100,000 in total fines in their first championship season in 1989. The first taste of champagne was well worth the trouble and the expense. "It was a relief when we won it," Laimbeer recalled, especially since the Pistons had come so painfully close to winning the two previous years.

When they won another championship in 1990, the Pistons proved you didn't have to be a collection of all-stars to be the best. For the second straight year, they were only the third team in league history to win a championship without having a player on the all-NBA team.

Their second title was a tribute to the Pistons' grit and determination, evoking that old chestnut: *The sum of the team is better than its parts*. "You've got to have mental toughness," said McCloskey, "and these guys did. That's the legacy right there."

Along with the physical toughness, of course.

"It's something that shouldn't be forgotten," said Dumars, who lasted several more years after the "Bad Boys" had gone their separate ways.

Those Pistons would be hard to forget.

Chicago's Scottie Pippen hits the floor after taking an elbow from Detroit's Bill Laimbeer during a playoff game.

THE HAMMER

Dave Schultz never met a brawl he didn't like to start. "Perhaps I got a little carried away with my role," Schultz said. "But nobody in the dressing room was complaining."

Broad Street Bullies enforcer Dave Schultz holds the record for the most penalty minutes in a season (472). Though he was loved in Philadelphia, he needed police escorts in many cities to protect him from screaming fans.

Schultz played the featured part of "The Hammer" in the long-running Philadelphia hit *The Broad Street Bullies*. In other words: Head Goon. Mr. Sluggo. Rambo on Ice.

Schultz holds the record for most penalty minutes in a season—472—and, at the time of his retirement in 1980, was the NHL's career leader with 2,294. He committed so many fouls he could have set up a cot in the penalty box. He averaged 4.29 minutes a night during his 535-game, eight-year NHL career with four teams. Only four players in league history had a higher per-game career average as the NHL began the 1999–2000 season.

Not exactly Mr. Nice Guy. But without Schultz's aggressive behavior—bordering on criminal, some said—the Broad Street Bullies would not have made their mark in NHL history. The combination of Schultz's nastiness on the ice and a group of highly skilled players helped the Flyers win Stanley Cups in 1974 and 1975 and advance to the finals in 1976.

"Schultz helped give our team a personality," captain Bobby Clarke said. "We became something our team had to live up to. We had a reputation, an image."

And, largely because of Schultz, it wasn't a very nice one. Schultz, who once attended Mennonite Bible camps in Saskatchewan, appeared to be the devil incarnate to fans wherever the Flyers played on the road.

"That's where I used to do most of my fighting," said Schultz, who amazingly was involved in twenty-six fights one season. "I can't believe the stuff I used to do. It was wild back then. Wild! And, wow, I was hated. The fans used to come out for one reason, and that was to see my butt get kicked."

At the Flyers' Spectrum arena, Schultz was a god. Schultz had his own "Schultz's Army" with fans coming to the game wearing World War II German helmets. Forget about *Hogan's Heroes*. The Flyers had their own "Sergeant Schultz."

Road games were a different story. Wherever the Flyers traveled, it was Schultz who usually bore the brunt of the fans' wrath. He actually needed police escorts in many cities to get him past fans screaming for his hide.

Schultz, a six foot one, 190 pounder out of Waldheim, Saskatchewan, was the Flyers' fifth choice, fifty-second overall, in the 1969 draft. A product of the Canadian Juniors, Schultz spent a couple of seasons in the minors and played in one Flyers game before they brought him up for good in the 1972–1973 season.

Although a good offensive player in the Juniors and Minors, Schultz created a new job description while playing with Roanoke in the old Eastern Hockey League. "I got into a couple of fights my first two games and did good, and it just went from there," Schultz said.

Schultz actually scored twenty goals in his second year with the Flyers, but coach Fred Shero already had him pigeon-holed. "I was what you'd call an 'enforcer,' but I prefer the term 'policeman,'" said Schultz. "I protected guys with my stick or my elbow. I was just doing what a lot of other guys in the league were doing. But did I take my role to the furthest possible extent? Close. Real close."

The Flyers' unruly behavior created such a backlash that the NHL was forced to change its rules regarding violence. While quietly considering its hard-hitting image part of its appeal, the NHL soon passed the instigator rule, penalizing players for provoking a fight.

That came in 1976 and it was no coincidence that the Flyers traded Schultz to the Los Angeles Kings the same year. Hockey was changing to a kinder, gentler sport, it seemed, and it was assumed that players like Schultz would be ineffective. The legislation might just as well have been called the "Dave Schultz Rule."

That was the beginning of the end for the Broad Street Bullies. For Schultz, it will be a never-ending memory. "We didn't back down from anybody," he said.

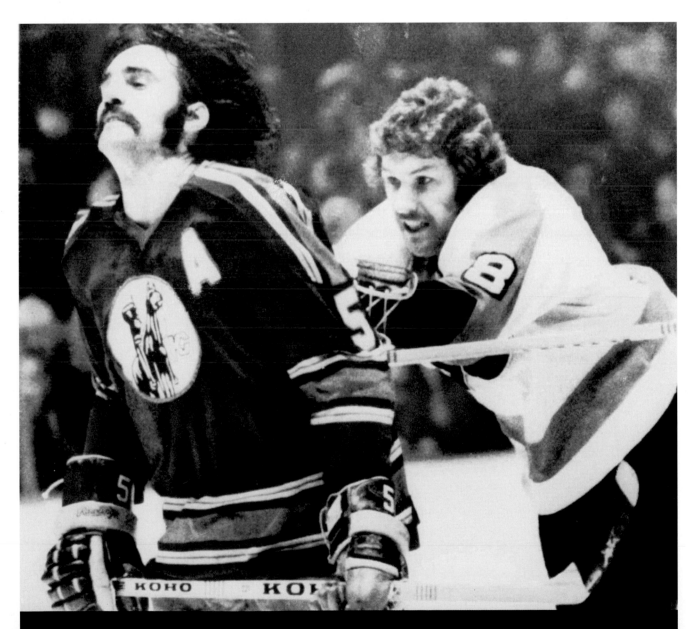

Dave Schultz and his team's unruly behavior created such a backlash that the NHL was forced to change its rules regarding violence. The NHL passed the instigator rule, which penalized players for provoking fights.

BIG, BAD BRUINS

They had nicknames like "The Chief," "The Turk," and "Swoop." In the early '70s, they held Boston in their grip and ruled the NHL with an iron hand.

They were called the "Big, Bad Bruins" by the media. And, proud of the image, they lived up to that ferocious nickname both on and off the ice.

If the Philadelphia Flyers set the standard for tough, two-fisted play in the NHL in the mid-'70s, they were only building on what the Boston Bruins had established a few years earlier. The Bruins broke the mold. Actually, they demolished it while winning Stanley Cups in 1970 and 1972.

The Bruins were an anomaly in their time, featuring both size and talent along with their mean-spirited play.

The organization had put together an incredible collection of skilled players highlighted by Bobby Orr on defense, Phil Esposito on offense, and Gerry Cheevers in goal. But it was the Bruins' intimidating, roughhouse style that expressed the team's personality. Hungry for a Stanley Cup after twenty-nine years, the Bruins during the 1969–1970 season seemed hell-bent on finding out the reason why they hadn't won for so *damn* long.

The hallmark of the Bruins was a group of big, rugged forwards with a hit-first-ask-questions-later philosophy. Phil Esposito, Ken Hodge, Derek "Turk" Sanderson, Wayne Cashman, Johnny "The Chief" Bucyk, Wayne "Swoop" Carleton and Ed Westfall were all six feet or over in height. They looked even bigger, and meaner, to the opposition in their black-dominated road uniforms. Like the Flyers, the rough and tumble Bruins engendered passionate loyalty at home and hate everywhere else.

They were easy to dislike, with their punishing style that often erupted into free-for-alls. Before a public outcry forced the NHL to rein in violence later in the '70s, a Bruins brawl was as common in the league as Orr's 100-point seasons.

"I only got hate letters," Sanderson said of his time with the Bruins.

He wasn't the only one, although Sanderson seemed destined to typify the "naughty-boy" behavior of the hard-drinking, hard-playing Bruins. At one point, the Bruins' No. 1 rogue confessed, "I was drinking a bottle and a half a day."

While punishing his body with alcohol and drugs, Sanderson was also punishing opposing players. In the 1972 playoffs, he set a Bruins record with seventy-two penalty minutes. "Everybody on that team had a role, and they fulfilled it," Sanderson said.

Like Cashman, who would drop his gloves as quickly as the puck was dropped. Here was talent with temper, and—by the way—no one was tougher going into the corners. "Cash was Cash," said Bruins defenseman Gary Doak. "He might have had his odd stuff off the ice such as destroying a Vancouver hotel room the day Esposito was traded to New York, but he really symbolized the Bruins. He was one of those hard-working, tough, good players."

Once arrested for driving while under the influence, Cashman was taken to the station house and given his one requisite phone call. No, he didn't call his lawyer: he sent out for Chinese food.

"The guys fooled around a lot, sure, but when the chips were down, guys pulled up their pants and played," said Ace Bailey, a rookie forward with the Bruins in the 1969–1970 season. "A lot of what we were doing isn't printable—but, trust me, it was crazy. We were everywhere together, all the watering holes, and we couldn't do anything wrong."

At least not in Boston, where long-suffering fans worshiped the god-like Bruins. And now they had a team to be proud of—at least, from their own perspective.

Just about every bumper sticker in Boston featured the irreverent line of the day: "Jesus Saves . . . and Esposito scores on the rebound." As great as Cashman was in the corners, Esposito was equally as good in front of the net. Of Esposito's 717 career goals with the Bruins, Chicago Blackhawks and New York Rangers, most of them were scored on rebounds, tips, or tap-ins where all the action—and danger—was. Like his teammates, the rugged Esposito gave as good as he got.

Usually playing with Cashman and Hodge, Esposito and his linemates accounted for a large portion of the Bruins' scoring. Another high-profile line: Johnny Bucyk, Fred Stanfield, and John "Pie Face" McKenzie. Amazingly, in the 1970–71 season those six, along with Orr, all finished in the top ten in NHL scoring.

Oddly, it was a season the heavily favored Bruins did not win the Cup, despite finishing with the NHL's best record at 57-14-7. Shockingly, the Bruins were knocked out in the first round by an upstart Montreal Canadiens team. Embarrassed by the upset, the swaggering Bruins came back the following season to claim the Cup they felt was rightfully theirs.

Ed Westfall, who later played with the New York Islanders and watched them win four straight Stanley Cups as a broadcaster, said the Bruins were a better team. Westfall pointed out that the Big, Bad Bruins could play any type of game, "whether it was the finesse game, the speed game, or the heavy-hitting game . . . We had guys who could fight, guys who could scrap, but all good hockey players," said Westfall.

A COSTLY INCIDENT

The U.S. men's hockey team figured to do some damage at the 1998 Nagano Olympics. They did, though it didn't happen on the ice.

After they had been eliminated by the Czech Republic, American players created an international incident by trashing one of the rooms in their living quarters.

This wasn't just any team. This was a group of "mature" professionals from the NHL making its first appearance in the Olympics, name players already known and admired around the world.

After the Games, they were known by only one name: Ugly Americans.

Not all of the Americans were guilty—actually, only a handful were. While most of the players were in bed, their quarters were being redecorated. Chairs were broken, walls sprayed with fire extinguishers, and pieces of chairs and a fire extinguisher were tossed off a fifth-floor balcony.

Total damage: $3,000. Damage to the Americans' reputation? Too high to measure.

Doug Weight, a member of the U.S. team, admitted that the players were "singing and drinking" after they

Members of the U.S. men's hockey team were named the Ugly Americans at the 1998 Nagano Olympics. After being eliminated from the competition, a handful of players broke chairs, tossed them off a balcony, and sprayed walls with fire extinguishers. Three thousand dollars in damages later, and with their tails between their legs, the team left before closing ceremonies.

The Americans couldn't work together as a team on the ice at Nagano, but when it came time to accept responsibility for their vandalism, they were quick to close ranks.

were eliminated and were "probably . . . too loud." But he thought the incident had been blown out of proportion by the media. "Just because we made noise and had a few beers doesn't mean we destroyed the village."

But, uh . . . Doug, what about the chairs? His answer hardly carried any weight. "Some of the guys were wrestling. We're big guys, and the chairs aren't that strong. Some broke just by sitting and playing cards."

America is a land of free speech. But there were few words forthcoming from the disgraced American players. No one came forward to admit his guilt and, suddenly, the team demonstrated a togetherness that had been absent on the ice. No one was squealing.

Meanwhile, the Czech Republic, led by Dominik Hasek, beat Russia in the gold medal game. The embarrassed U.S. hockey team didn't stick around for the closing ceremonies.

Not even a check for $3,000 and a generic apology by U.S. captain Chris Chelios to Japanese Olympic officials two months later could assuage the damage that had been done.

Americans had always viewed their teams as the good guys wearing the white hats in international events. But this time even the most patriotic saw the American hockey team wearing black hats, and U.S. sports wearing a black eye

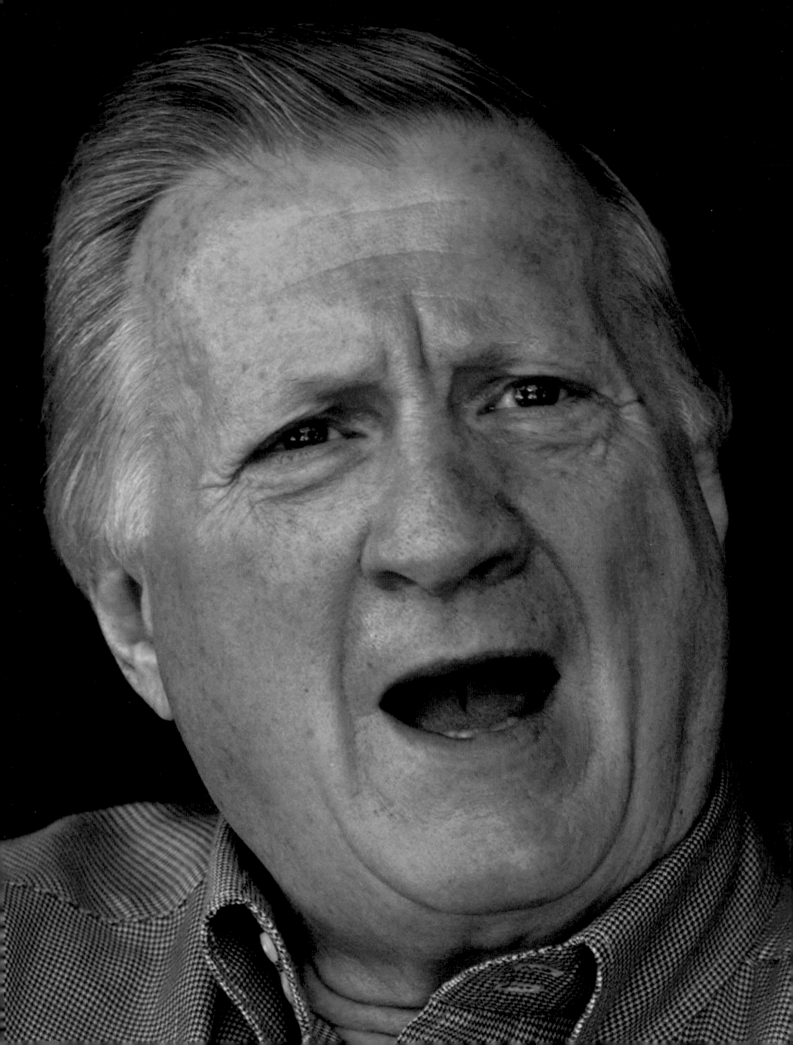

NO YANKEE DOODLE DANDY

It isn't only the sluggers, skaters, and slam-dunkers who sometimes earn infamy along with their huge salaries. In some instances, the people who pay those salaries believe their positions of power and wealth entitle them to act just as antisocially.

Try George Steinbrenner in New York, for one. Marge Schott in Cincinnati for another. And Walter O'Malley, who gave Brooklyn the Bum's Rush.

Few team owners have done more to create angst and anger than this unholy trio in baseball.

They don't have a corner on the market, either. So meet the moguls of menace.

George Steinbrenner could have been a local hero in a New York Minute. They would have erected a statue outside Yankee Stadium and renamed the Bronx after him.

He could have gotten his own day, preferably on the Fourth of July, when this Yankee Doodle Dandy was actually born. Joe DiMaggio Highway? What about Steinbrenner Street?

Under his ownership, the Yankees recaptured their esteem, once more becoming baseball's most dominant club. They won four American League pennants in six years, and the 1977 and 1978 World Series. More recently, the Yanks won the Series in 1996, 1998 and 1999, yet another golden era.

Yet Steinbrenner is more vilified than venerated. How could a man whose team has had such success be more loathed than loved?

For George M. Steinbrenner, the formula has been complex, with doses of outrageousness and

Under George Steinbrenner's ownership, the Yankees won the 1977, 1978, 1996, 1998, and 1999 World Series. And the staff changes have been equally impressive: twenty managerial changes in twenty-five years, general managers fired fifteen times, pitching coaches fired nearly forty times, and thirteen (and still counting) public relations directors dismissed.

STEINBRENNER'S FOLLIES

- Steinbrenner criticized Jim Abbott, the pitcher born without a right hand who became a major league star, for making too many in-season charity appearances. He claimed it led to poor pitching by Abbott.

  "I meet kids in New York and on the road who might face the same type of challenges I faced," Abbott said. "I think I owe those kids ten or fifteen minutes . . . and I'm not going to change."

  Soon, he was a former Yankee.

- Steinbrenner twice ordered publicist Marty Appel to take overnight flights back from the West Coast so Appel could be at his post in Yankee Stadium the next morning to receive Steinbrenner's phone call, only the Boss didn't bother to call.

  Larry Wahl, one of Appel's successors, was ordered to recall 12,000 copies of the 1980 Yankees yearbook because Steinbrenner's lips were too red in his full-page photo.

  "On most teams, the job is crazy," said Harvey Greene, who lasted three years under Steinbrenner, mainly because Greene might be the best publicist in sports. "On the Yankees, it's deranged. My yearly goal was to see my house once during daylight hours."

- Commissioner Bowie Kuhn fined him for tampering with a college player, Billy Cannon, Jr., just months after Steinbrenner took control.

- Dick Howser guided the Yanks to a 103-59 record, only their best record in Steinbrenner's reign. But they didn't win the pennant in 1980 and Howser was fired after one season as manager. The owner claimed Howser no longer wanted to be a manager. A few weeks later, the Royals hired Howser as manager.

- A year later, after his team lost Game 5 of the World Series in Los Angeles, Steinbrenner announced he had fought off two twentysomething Dodgers fans in an elevator.

  "I clocked them," he said. "There are two guys in this town probably looking for teeth."

  The story was met with much skepticism, because Steinbrenner rarely ventured into out-of-town elevators—or anywhere else—without a bodyguard.

- Steinbrenner swore that Berra would manage the entire 1985 season. By Game 16, Yogi, as revered as any Yankee, was gone and swore never to set foot in Yankee Stadium as long as Steinbrenner owns the team. He stuck to that edict for thirteen years.

  For the 1990 Oldtimers Game, Yogi Berra, Mickey Mantle and Reggie Jackson—all Yankee greats— were absent.

George Steinbrenner talks with members of the press
at Yankee Stadium in New York April 25, 1974.

meanness, insensitivity and indignance, felonies and misdemeanors. In the end, Steinbrenner's legacy won't be the championships so much as how he mistreated employees, alienated peers, and turned a franchise known for its glorious history into something of a laughing stock.

The Bronx Zoo, indeed.

Asked how he could tell when Steinbrenner was lying, White Sox owner Jerry Reinsdorf, an equally powerful force in baseball, said, "That's easy, his lips are moving."

Asked how deep Steinbrenner's knowledge of the game is, former Yankees manager Dallas Green replied, "He doesn't know a damn thing about the game of baseball."

Asked about working for The Boss, star first baseman Don Mattingly—the most popular Yankee of the last twenty years—said, "You come here and get no respect. They treat you like crap. They belittle your performance and make you look bad in the media. After they give you the money, it doesn't matter to them. They think they can do whatever they want. They think money is respect."

Steinbrenner didn't spend a whole lot to buy the Yankees, who lay almost dormant during CBS' nine-year ownership. He paid ten million dollars in 1973 for a franchise that entered the new millennium worth perhaps thirty times that.

Upon purchasing the most storied of franchises, Steinbrenner, raised in Cleveland and a native of Tampa, promised he "won't be active in the day-to-day operations of the club." Instead, he has been active minute-by-minute.

Active as in *meddling, intrusive,* unfairly *demanding.* He has managed to estrange the likes of Yogi Berra and Dave Winfield, two great players. He has threatened to move the team not only out of the Bronx, but out of New York entirely.

Unprecedented players salaries were not the only money issues to haunt the Yankees owner. Linked to a plot that sounded like something from *The Sopranos,* claims of hush money surrounded Steinbrenner.

His impatience has led to twenty managerial changes in twenty-five years—Billy Martin had the job five times. Steinbrenner has fired general managers fifteen times, pitching coaches nearly forty times, and has had thirteen public relations directors—that is, if he hasn't fired someone in the last week or so.

Gene Legatt took over as team president on

September 19, 1988, was berated by Steinbrenner three days later, and quit within twenty-four hours.

"It's tough working for me. I know that," Steinbrenner once said. "I admit I'm tough on my people. I'm tough on myself."

Steinbrenner himself was absent from running the team on two occasions. Nothing provides a more enlightening view of the man who has praised Attila the Hun than his involvement with Richard Nixon's re-election campaign, and with a gambler named Howard Spira.

A major contributor to the Republican Party, Steinbrenner was a backer of Nixon's 1972 campaign. Yes, that one. While Steinbrenner had nothing to do with the Watergate break-in that brought down the Nixon Administration, he was indicted on fifteen counts of election law violations.

Steinbrenner could have spent fifty-five years in prison.

He originally pleaded not guilty to all fifteen counts, then entered a guilty plea to one count of conspiracy to make illegal campaign contributions. He was fined $15,000 by a Cleveland federal court, then was suspended by baseball commissioner Bowie Kuhn for two years.

Steinbrenner also was charged with forcing employees of his American Ship Building Company to lie to FBI agents and a grand jury. He vehemently denied those charges and never was convicted.

Kuhn later shortened the sentence to fifteen months, and The Boss was back on March 1, 1976, in time to oversee his first pennant.

Two years later, Billy Martin would be fired for his caustic criticism of Steinbrenner and outfielder Reggie Jackson: "One is convicted and the other is a liar."

Steinbrenner's second suspension was the result of an ugly management-labor incident, one of the worst baseball has ever seen.

Ever the star-worshipper, Steinbrenner signed primo free agent Dave Winfield to an unprecedented ten-year, twenty-three million dollar contract (remember, this was in 1980)—although The Boss mistakenly believed it would cost him only seventeen million. Soon, Steinbrenner would be disparaging Winfield as "Mr. May" because he couldn't match Jackson's postseason heroics. Who could?

Steinbrenner sought ways to get out of the contract, at one point accusing Winfield of mismanaging a charitable foundation. The Boss withheld his annual $450,000 payment to the fund. In the most egregious of plots, he hired Howard Spira, who was in heavy debt due to gambling losses, to collect damaging information on Winfield.

Eventually, Steinbrenner paid Spira $40,000, claiming it was to stop Spira from harassing Steinbrenner's family and friends. Kindly George also insisted he paid because Spira's mother was ill with cancer and Spira's father needed the money to repay loans from neighbors.

Others believed it was hush money to keep Spira from making public taped conversations and from making embarrassing accusations about former Yankees manager Lou Piniella, former stadium manager Pat Kelly, and M. David Weidler, another former Yankees official.

"If it's extortion, coercion or blackmail, I don't know the difference of these terms," The Boss said. "I probably never will. I can only tell you how it felt. I was deeply concerned, apprehensive about what this guy was going to do to me and my family."

Fearing he would lose his vice presidency on the U.S. Olympic Committee if suspended by baseball, Steinbrenner agreed to resign as managing general partner of the Yankees in August 1990. Commissioner Fay Vincent was prepared to suspend him for two years.

By March 1, 1993, Steinbrenner was back running the Yankees. Meet the new Boss, same as the old Boss.

"He doesn't want anyone around he can't command," Green said. "He wants a puppet machine."

SCHOTTZIE

It might be unfair to say all of the Cincinnati Reds believed owner Marge Schott treated her dogs better than her players.

Of course, if those players were Latinos or Jewish or Asian, they probably knew how lowly Schott regarded them. Schott, who suffered from chronic foot-in-mouth disease, was regarded as an equal-opportunity bigot.

"I don't think Marge has anything against any one group of people or race," Pete Rose said. "I just don't

Cincinnati Reds owner Marge Schott (center), with the aid of Reds Publicity Director Jon Braude (right), lets out a yell as she makes her way through a large group of media representatives at the team's training camp in Plant City, Florida.

think she likes anybody." Anyone, that is, other than Schottzie and Schottzie II, her St. Bernards to whom she gave free reign at Riverfront Stadium—even on the field, where they often left a trail.

On the day before Christmas 1984, Schott became the team's majority owner. Having inherited much of her fortune, she knew little about business, much less baseball. Reds president Bob Howsam, who convinced Schott to buy the team when it appeared it might be moved out of Cincinnati, said, "It turned out to be the worst thing I've ever done in baseball."

Even in her greatest moment, when the Reds swept the vaunted Oakland Athletics to win the 1990 World Series, she fumed because team owners don't begin making most of their money until the Series reaches five games. So, Schott refused to underwrite a team party.

During that Series, star outfielder Eric Davis injured a kidney while making a spectacular diving catch. Schott refused to provide Davis with a medically equipped airplane for his return to Cincinnati, reasoning that her "over-paid" players made enough money to handle such expenses themselves.

While Schott was popular among Cincinnatians for keeping the club in the Queen City, for bringing back Rose as manager, and for sitting amongst the fans at Riverfront rather than in her private box, she was an embarrassment for the sport.

Schott sat in the stands smoking cigarettes even after it was outlawed at the stadium. To save $350 a month, she dropped the service that provided out-of-town scores on the scoreboard, wondering why fans cared about a game other than the one they were watching.

She fired one of her best managers, Davey Johnson, because she disapproved of his girlfriend.

She cut the Reds' scouting and minor league development staffs so severely the team couldn't compete for years. Her reasoning? "All they do is sit and watch baseball games."

When umpire John McSherry dropped dead early in the opening game of the 1996 season, she complained that the game was postponed. "Can't they play with two umpires?" she asked, fretting that a sellout crowd was sent home. The next day, she sent flowers to the umpires—second-hand flowers that were sent to her for the opener.

But by far the worst of Marge's utterances and actions were the ones that marked her as a racist.

Eric Davis and Dave Parker, two of her finest players, were referred to as "million dollar niggers." During a telephone conversation, she was heard saying, "I would never hire another nigger. I'd rather have a trained monkey working for me than a nigger."

Her insensitive language at times included the words "kike," "Jap," and "spic," and she publicly disparaged various ethnic groups.

In 1993, Schott was suspended by Major League Baseball for a year. She was fined $25,000 and ordered to attend multicultural training programs.

Clearly, she didn't learn, condemning the earring wearers among the Reds as "fruits," and admitting that she kept a swastika in her desk drawer. Schott also claimed that Hitler "was good at the beginning, but he just went too far."

Schott had gone too far. In June 1996, she agreed to surrender daily control of the Reds after baseball's executive council threatened her with a lengthy suspension.

The next year she was accused of using the names of Reds employees to falsify records to reach sales quotas at her Chevrolet dealership. Under federal investigation, she agreed to sell the dealership.

By late 1998, Schott was forced to sell her majority stake in the Reds. As the '99 season began, baseball was finally rid of the scourge of Cincinnati.

Marge Schott's irreverence knew no bounds. If she wasn't insulting some ethnic group,
then it was one of her players. She once said she loved dogs because
"they never talk back" and "never ask for a raise."

BROOKLYN'S BIGGEST BUM

No team ever has or possibly ever will have the symbiotic relationship the Dodgers had with Brooklyn. They were "Dem Bums," but to every Brooklynite they were "Our Bums," beloved from Flatbush to Bensonhurst, worshipped from Coney Island to Williamsburg.

When they didn't win the World Series—it wasn't for lack of opportunity, either—their loyal fans cried, then shrugged, and said "Wait 'til next year." When the Dodgers finally won the World Series in 1955, Brooklyn threw a party worthy of Mardi Gras, New Year's Eve, and VE Day combined.

And when Walter O'Malley broke every Brooklynite's heart by taking their sporting lifeblood away, he was called everything from Judas' kid to the Devil incarnate.

Long before O'Malley began the major league exodus westward, dragging the New York Giants along with

Dodgers owner Walter O'Malley stands between county supervisor Kenneth Hahn and City councilwomen Rosalind Wyman as he stepped from a private plane marked "Los Angeles Dodgers" to a huge civic welcome at LA's International Airport on October 23, 1957.

him to California, he'd built a reputation for nastiness. Although O'Malley was known for lavishing his players and other employees with superb working conditions, he was also a tyrant who tried to steal credit from underlings who deserved it.

O'Malley was a mortgage forecloser (which probably says enough about his soft spots) when the Brooklyn Trust Company took control of the team in 1942. O'Malley was put in charge and immediately began feuding with Larry MacPhail, whose free-spending—he put lights on Ebbets Field and refurbished it, then hired Red Barber as radio announcer—irked the bottom-line O'Malley. When MacPhail joined the army in 1942, O'Malley seized the opportunity and bought twenty-five percent of the Dodgers.

Another part owner, Branch Rickey, handled the baseball operations, putting together an enviable minor league system and scouting staff. Then Rickey set about breaking the color barrier by recruiting Jackie Robinson to become the first black player in the majors.

While O'Malley never opposed it, he didn't exactly encourage Rickey or Robinson. Robinson, in fact, said O'Malley was

Walter O'Malley was the consummate businessman, always concerned with the bottom line. After the Dodgers won the 1949 pennant, O'Malley refused to order World Series rings until the players returned the ones they had received two years earlier.

"viciously antagonistic" toward him. In 1951, Robinson complained about being assigned to stay in a blacks-only hotel on a road trip. O'Malley's reply? "A separate hotel was good enough for you in 1947."

"To put it bluntly," Robinson wrote in his autobiography, "I was one of those uppity niggers in O'Malley's book."

Yet, years later, O'Malley claimed it was his idea, not Rickey's, to integrate the major leagues.

After the Dodgers won the 1949 pennant, O'Malley refused to order World Series rings until the players returned their rings from 1947. The next year he bought out Rickey, first offering only the original $350,000 Rickey invested seven years earlier, even though the Dodgers had made nearly three million dollars in profits. Rickey was able to walk away with about one million only because of some legal technicalities.

In subsequent years, O'Malley would fire popular manager Burt Shotton, who was hired by Rickey; impose a one-dollar fine on any Dodgers employee ever mentioning Rickey's name; and hide his negotiations with Los Angeles even as he sought a new stadium in Brooklyn.

Then, in 1957, O'Malley dropped the bombshell: the Dodgers were leaving for the West Coast. Brooklynites wouldn't build a stadium for O'Malley, one of New York's richest men. Baseball was a business. The Dodgers were a business.

The diehard fans didn't matter. The rich tradition of Dem Bums didn't matter. Money mattered. California was paved with gold.

The announcement stunned the sports world. In Brooklyn, tears flowed. The Dodgers' switchboard was flooded. So was City Hall's. Had talk radio existed then, every caller would have been expressing outrage.

O'Malley merely shrugged, packed up his team, and headed west. He could never dare set foot in Brooklyn again, though he didn't seem to care.

Years later, several Brooklynites compiled a list of the worst humans in history. Right behind Hitler and Stalin was Walter O'Malley.

VILLANOUS OWNERS

They pay the bills, therefore they can make their own rules. At least that's how these villainous owners behaved:

• **George Preston Marshall.** The founder of the Washington Redskins was one of pro football's most reactionary owners. Considered the NFL's leading racist, Marshall's team was the last to integrate (1962).

Marshall so antagonized the Chicago Bears with his comments after a Redskins victory that the Bears got their vengeance with a 73-0 romp in the 1940 championship game. Redskins star Sammy Baugh claims his teammates were so angry with Marshall that they allowed the Bears to run up the score.

• **Bob Irsay.** On a snowy spring night in 1984, after the state of Maryland voted to give Baltimore the power to take over the Colts through eminent domain—the city offered forty million dollars for the franchise—Irsay loaded up the moving vans. He ended his dispute with municipal authorities over building a new stadium by relocating to Indianapolis.

Irsay destroyed a thirty-year pro football tradition in Baltimore; the bitterness lasted decades.

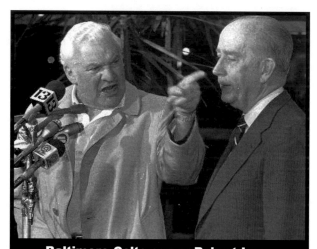

Baltimore Colts owner Robert Irsay engages in a shouting match with reporters during a news conference where Irsay denied making a deal to move the National Football League franchise to Phoenix.

• **Art Modell.** Taking a cue from Irsay, and spurred on by the largesse of, yes, the city of Baltimore, Modell moved the Browns out of Cleveland. He announced the transfer in the middle of the 1995 season, ruining any chance for the Browns to win that year. Other NFL owners, powerless to stop the move, so disapproved of Modell abandoning such a football stronghold that they agreed to give Cleveland an expansion team.

Modell never set foot in Cleveland again, a wise move considering the animosity that still exists.

• **Jerry Reinsdorf.** The hard-line owner of the Chicago White Sox was a leading cause of the 1994 strike that forced cancellation of the World Series and sent major league baseball reeling for years. He also had a major role in the 1998–1999 NBA lockout that nearly ruined the season, then oversaw the breakup of the six-time champion Chicago Bulls, who went from Invinci-Bulls to Unwatcha-Bulls.

• **John Spano/Steven Gluckstern, Howard Millstein, Stephen Ross, and Dan Doctoroff.** This group bought the New York Islanders in 1998 after Spano had duped the NHL into approving him as owner even though he had almost no capital. Spano wound up with a six-year jail term, but the new owners didn't do Islanders fans any favors, either.

Gluckstern's group immediately demanded that Nassau County build a new arena for the team that won four straight Stanley Cups in the 1980s. When that ploy failed, they began selling off or trading the team's best and most expensive players. By the 1999–2000 season, what was left had the look of a minor-league outfit playing in an outmoded arena that was nearly empty most nights. A once-proud franchise had been shamed.

- **Harry Frazee.** In 1918, the Boston Red Sox won the World Series. A year later, owner Harry Frazee sold Babe Ruth, one of the best pitchers in the game and a blossoming hitter, to the hated New York Yankees. Frazee needed money to finance a Broadway show and got $80,000 for Ruth, who merely turned into the greatest slugger and most popular player in the national pastime. The so-called "Curse of the Bambino" has haunted the Red Sox, who have played second-best to the Yankees ever since.

- **Nelson Skalbania/Peter Pocklington.** The men who greedily traded or sold Wayne Gretzky. Skalbania signed a seventeen-year-old Gretzky in 1978 for the Indianapolis Racers of the WHA. After eight games, Skalbania sold Gretzky's personal services contract to Edmonton.

  Ten years later, after Gretzky ascended to the top of the hockey world and carried the Oilers with him, Pocklington traded him to the Los Angeles Kings because he could no longer afford "The Great One." It was as if a Canadian treasure had been lost—sent to the United States, no less—and Pocklington received ten million dollars in the deal, to boot.

- **Bruce McNall/Jeffrey Sudikoff.** The former co-owners of the Kings and the guys who brought Gretzky to LA weren't such do-gooders after all. McNall pleaded guilty to defrauding banks of $236 million and wound up in jail. Sudikoff was found guilty of insider training and fined three million dollars in addition to a jail sentence.

- **Charlie Finley.** One of the game's great showmen, Finley makes the list only because he once tried to fire second baseman Mike Andrews during the World Series after Andrews made two errors. And for the fact that Finley dismantled his team when huge salaries and free agency loomed in the 1970s.

  His Oakland A's dynasty self-destructed when Finley allowed superstars such as Reggie Jackson, Catfish Hunter, and Vida Blue to get away. He even attempted to sell Blue to the Yankees and Joe Rudi and Rollie Fingers to the Red Sox in 1976, but commissioner Bowie Kuhn blocked him. Finley eventually conducted a fire sale for those high-priced vets who hadn't yet walked away.

Oakland Athletics owner Charlie O. Finley speaks to the media at Baseball Commissioner Bowie Kuhn's office in New York. Kuhn called a hearing because Finley planned to sell All-Stars Rollie Fingers, Vida Blue, and Joe Rudi.

DRUG DEMONS

It's not just hits, runs, and errors any more. The lexicon of modern sports also includes phrases such as performance enhancers, anabolic steroids, recreational drugs, beta blockers, and urine tests. Such language now takes up a major portion of the Olympic dictionary, and is the most serious issue with which the Games must deal. Not to mention sports in general.

Ben Johnson's shameful story is the flashpoint for all that is negative about the ugly world of drugs in sports. Johnson has plenty of company in the flaunting of the rules. Olympic teams from East Germany and China have been caught red-handed, as has baseball's Steve Howe, Darryl Strawberry and Dwight Gooden.

They aren't the only troubled athletes. Welcome to the dark side of sports. Uh, enter at your own risk.

It had the air of a heavyweight championship fight, a Super Bowl, and the World Cup final rolled together. It would last less than ten seconds, yet it would be the most memorable event at the 1988 Summer Olympics.

For years, Ben Johnson and Carl Lewis were the most bitter—not to mention the fastest—rivals in sports. Over the final months leading to Seoul, their feud had been carried out on the track, in the media, and by fans of the Canadian and American super sprinters.

On Saturday, September 24, Lewis seemed relaxed, almost giddy, as he warmed up for the 100-meter final that would establish the winner as the World's Fastest Human. Lewis won the title four years earlier at the Los Angeles Olympics, but Johnson had since surpassed the U.S. star.

This race would be the ultimate proving ground for both. And while Lewis smiled during warmups, his natural adrenalin flowing, Johnson appeared

"What Ben did is superhuman," said hurdles gold medalist Roger Kingdom. And he was right. Ben Johnson enhanced his natural talents with anabolic steroids.

grim, deep in concentration, almost in a trance.

Something else was flowing within him.

As they crouched in the starting blocks, Johnson's taut leg, arm, and shoulder muscles bulged out of his track suit. He had the look of a weightlifter or bodybuilder, nothing like the lithe Lewis.

Johnson exploded out of the blocks. Lewis looked over to see Johnson a few steps ahead of him midway through the race. He was shocked to see Johnson maintain the speed.

And the world was thrilled when the time 9.79 flashed on the scoreboard. Ben Johnson not only won the most prestigious track event on the planet, he shattered the world record of 9.83 seconds.

"What Ben did is superhuman," said hurdles gold medalist Roger Kingdom.

Kingdom was right. Johnson's record was not achieved naturally, through hard work and determination. It was gained supernaturally, through drugs and cheating.

A day and a half after his magnificent run, Johnson was stripped of his gold medal and world record and left Seoul in disgrace. His urine samples showed huge dosages of stanozolol, a banned anabolic steroid that artifically increases muscle mass and strength and shortens the recovery time between workouts.

Johnson and his entourage would make the claim that drugs were administered when someone tampered with his post-race drink. The sophisticated testing machines said otherwise, indicating the usual pattern of drug use by athletes.

"From the analysis of the data, it's quite evident that the drug was administered a few times prior to the Games and interruption of treatment took

After months of rigorous training and a well calculated program of steroid use, Ben Johnson leads the pack to win the 100-meter dash final in Seoul.

place some days and perhaps some weeks before the event," said Dr. Robert Dugal, a Canadian member of the IOC medical commission.

Helped by his personal physician, Dr. Jamie Astaphan, Johnson undertook a well-calculated program of steroid supplements months before he set a world record in 1987. With such triumphs—and the feeling of invincibility that resulted from not having been caught—Johnson continued with this formula for success until just before the Seoul Games.

"He knew what he was taking," Astaphan told an inquiry into the use of performance-enhancing drugs by Canadian athletes.

Added Canadian Olympic sprinter Angella Issajenko, who was treated by Astaphan and trained with the same coach, Charlie Francis: "I'm fed up with all the bull . . . Ben takes steroids. I take steroids. Jamie [Astaphan] gives them to us. Charlie isn't a scientist, but he knows what's happening."

Francis would later document drug use by dozens of his athletes, as well as by others around the world.

"We're awash in a sea of denials," said Francis, whose comments inexplicably made him a pariah among his peers. "People have to recognize what's going on out there, admit that the levels of performance are not possible without performance-enhancing drugs, and get on with the process of trying to make some changes."

Johnson's humiliation was matched by the embarrassment of IOC members, most notably the organization's president, Juan Antonio Samaranch. In a heated response to the scandal, Samaranch equated athletic cheaters to outlaws and killers.

"Doping equals death," Samaranch said. "Alas, the thieves of sports performance, like their criminal counterparts in society, are forever striving to find new methods, often assisted by specialists who attach little importance to their oath or code of ethics they are supposed to respect."

While track and field has been plagued by drug

A banner hanging from the balcony in Seoul during the 1998 Summer Olympics sums up Ben Johnsons' career: "From Hero to Zero in 9.79."

scandals for decades—each year athletes are suspended for using performance-enhancers—none has been as earth-shattering as Ben Johnson's. Not only did he betray his event, his sport and the Olympic ideal, overshadowing all of the brilliant and uplifting performances at the Seoul Games, but he duped an entire country into idolizing him. Johnson was Canada's biggest hero on that early autumn day when he won the gold medal.

And he broke Canada's heart when it was stripped away.

Prime Minister Brian Mulroney said Johnson's disqualification was "a moment of great sorrow for all Canadians." Added Sports Minister Jean Charest, "A few days ago, Canada had the opportunity of having a great day of national pride. Then, we were shattered. Johnson knew what the rules were."

Ah, the rules! Do athletes who use performance-enhancing drugs care about the rules? Of course not.

Do they care that fans pay to see fair competitions?

Do they consider their status as role models, idols, heroes? Never. Winning at all costs is all that matters to them.

Dr. Robert Voy, the former chief medical officer for the USOC, believes Johnson's mindset is typical of most drug users.

"I suspect that Johnson just got greedy," Voy wrote in *Drugs, Sport and Politics*, "and thought he could take an extra dose of stanozolol and get away with it. Before Seoul, Johnson knew that he and Lewis probably would compete in the fastest 100-meter dash in history. He also knew that winning the race would mean millions of dollars, fame, and a better way of life.

"This was Johnson's once-in-a-lifetime shot, and the importance of that competition was just too much for him not to take the gamble. Besides, in over eight years of anabolid-androgenic steroid use, he had never been caught before."

When Johnson was caught, the firestorm that enveloped track and field and the Olympics swept the globe. The International Olympic Committee and its medical commission immediately promised more frequent testing with state-of-the-art equipment. Violators would face stronger suspensions—including, in the most egregious cases, lifetime bans.

The IAAF, the governing body for track and field, stripped all of Johnson's medals, titles, and records. Johnson was suspended from all competition for two years.

"What he did is against the rules, the ethics of sport, and it's bloody cheating," said Sebastian Coe, a two-time Olympic 1,500-meter champion and, in 1988, a member of the IOC's athletes commission. "You are either in the war or you are not."

But is this a war the "good guys" can win? Many experts wonder, because technology for masking drug usage is just as advanced as technology for detecting it. Each year cheaters find new performance-enhancers to make them run faster, jump higher, lift more, or last longer. And by the time the drug police develop ways of identifying the latest drug, the culprits have moved on to something even more advanced. And more lethal.

Beside not being fair or legal, drugs have many other drawbacks. Stanozolol, Johnson's chosen steroid, can cause liver damage and cancer.

"It makes you more aggressive in training," Dugal said. "There is some data that indicates steroids lead to major psychological disturbances and even criminal behavior in certain cases."

What Johnson did was criminal, and it landed him in an athletic limbo from which he never escaped. He lost millions of dollars in endorsements. He lost his medals and world records. He lost his self-respect as well as the respect of his fans.

A banner hanging from one balcony in the Seoul athletes' village summed it up:

"From Hero to Zero in 9.79."

WOMEN'S SWIM TEAMS

Drug use is not gender-proof, as the sad cases from East Germany and China prove. Such incredible East German swimmers as Kristin Otto, Barbara Krause, and Petra Thumer had their performances tainted by drug allegations. Otto won four individual gold medals and two in relays at the 1988 Olympics. She also took eight individual world titles. Krause, who missed the 1976 Games with what was reported as angina, won two golds at the 1980 Olympics. Thumer, fifteen at the time, replaced Krause for the 400 freestyle in 1976 at Montreal and won in a world record time that would have placed her second in the men's event. She also won the 800 in world record time.

Throughout the 1970s and 1980s, swimmers from the United States and other countries claimed the Germans were doped up. Were they sore losers? Their suspicions were later proved correct when East German swimmers, trainers, doctors, and coaches admitted to using unethical means to achieve success.

China succeeded East Germany as the dominant force in the pool, beginning with its divers in 1988. Led by Fu Mingxia (The Flying Fu), China produced teenage champions in both the springboard and platform events.

At the incredibly young age of eleven, Fu won a gold medal in the 10-meter platform at the 1990 Goodwill Games. She then won world titles in 1991 and 1994 and platform gold in the 1992 and 1996 Olympics. She also took the springboard crown in 1996.

Her secret? Hard work. In the ten hours she trained each day, Fu would perform 1,000 board exercises, rarely skipping a day, much less an hour of practice.

The Chinese divers were never accused of being anything more than precocious. Chinese swimmers, however, fell into a whirlpool of drug charges.

"We all talk about how manly they are," said American Kristine Quance. "Everyone knows about the allegations. Its obviously not been proven yet, but it's really frustrating."

Kristin Otto

Barbara Krause

Added Dave Haller, former coach of Britain's national swim team:

"I cannot see any other way they can come from oblivion to total domination of the world in such a short period. It has all the hallmarks of East Germany, unfortunately. It's all rather sad and I hope it can be resolved. Talking about drugs is very frustrating. But the whole swimming world is very frustrated by this."

Including the clean Chinese swimmers, who had built an impressive resume lined with gold, silver, and bronze at major international meets.

"When the U.S. or Europeans win, you don't accuse them," said star swimmer Le Jingyi. "Now that China's making a name for itself, everyone's talking about doping. I think it's all just jealousy."

Perhaps, in part. But there was also evidence of cheating, as drug scandals cast a pall over the Chinese program throughout the 1990s.

At the 1994 Asian Games, seven Chinese swimmers tested positive for steroids. In 1998, four Chinese tested positive for banned substances at the World Championships in Perth, Australia, and, in the most embarrassing of drug-related incidents, one was caught with vials of human growth hormone in her luggage.

Suspicion of steroid use by China's swimmers hit a high in 1992 at the Barcelona Olympics. FINA, the international swimming federation, tested randomly then, taking just two of the top four finishers. When Yong Zhuang won the 100 freestyle, she was not chosen for a test. American, Australian, and other coaches protested, saying Yong's deep voice and heavy muscles were indications of steroid use.

The United States and Australia, each of which would host an Olympics after Barcelona, pushed for more stringent testing; FINA finally complied in 1996.

Le Jingyi of China wins the gold medal in the womens 100 meter freestyle at the Georgia Tech Aquatic Center at the 1996 Centennial Olympic Games in Atlanta, Georgia.

China didn't fare nearly as well in Atlanta. Was it coincidence?

To its credit, China's state-run federation appointed a full-time antidoping official and made the award of cash prizes dependent on staying drug-free for four years.

Still, questions persisted about the likes of Le Jingyi, Le Lin, and Yong Zhuang, the stars of 1988, 1992, and 1996.

At the 1997 National Games in Shanghai, China's record-shattering performances by runners, weightlifters, and swimmers once again caught the sporting world's attention.

"They are obviously cheating—they are machines," Susan O'Neill, Australia's 1996 Olympic champion in the 200 meter butterfly, said of the Chinese swimmers. Unfortunately, by then such accusations had become a common complaint.

"If a Chinese swims fast, it's drugs. If a Chinese swims slowly, no drugs," said swimming coach Zhang Xiong. "It's not fair."

Perhaps the Chinese swimmers suffered from the scandal that surrounded their countrywomen running under coach Ma Junren.

Ma's training philosophy was, to say the very least, unconventional. He claimed his students ran about forty miles a day, a total unheard of by Western training standards, attributing his runner's success to high-altitude training and a special diet of herbal tonics, turtle blood soup, and caterpillar fungus.

Others claimed they were using performance-enhancing drugs.

"The rumors about my athletes being on drugs are created by the Western media," Ma said. "I welcome drug-testing on my runners at any time and, when the experts find all my athletes innocent, they can shut up and remove the bias against Chinese athletes."

Questions arose once Ma's runners proved inconsistent in competition. Several of his former students said he burned them out with his strict training methods; others said they were forced to drink his concoctions and had no idea what they were being given.

Ma fought back by saying that Western countries had been using drugs to boost the performances of their athletes for decades, but escaped being caught because of superior technology.

"Once they find a better drug, they use it to boost performance and put the old one on the banned list. That's why they don't break the law," he said.

Ma never could explain why, after their superb performances at the 1997 Chinese Games, his women failed to win a single individual medal at the world championships later that year.

The shame of it all is that, while women's teams were performing as well or better than men in so many sports, their world had become just as tainted by drug allegations. In that regard, equality came much too soon.

Ma Junren, Chinese track coach, at the 1994 Asian Games in Hiroshima, Japan.

DRUG DEMONS

The Ben Johnson scandal is the most infamous in the history of drug use. Steve Howe's case probably is the lengthiest, although Darryl Strawberry's comes close.

Here are some others who betrayed their sports, themselves, and the public with their drug use:

Lyle Alzado

- **Lyle Alzado.** Used steroids throughout his NFL career and died at age forty-three from brain cancer caused by the steroids.

- **Len Bias.** Celebrating being chosen second overall in the 1986 NBA draft by the Boston Celtics, the twenty-two-year-old Maryland All-American overdosed on cocaine and died.

- **Curtis Strong.** The caterer and former clubhouse cook for the Pittsburgh Pirates was convicted in 1985 of being a "traveling salesman of cocaine" to major league players.

- In 1983, Miami Dolphins star running back **Mercury Morris** was sentenced to twenty years in prison for distributing cocaine. That same year, NFL players E. J. Junior, Greg Stemrick, Ross Browner, and Pete Johnson were suspended four games each for possessing cocaine. In 1986, Cleveland safety Don Rogers died of a cocaine overdose.

- On the eve of the 1989 Super Bowl, **Stanley Wilson** of the Cincinnati Bengals was found in his hotel room in a drug-induced stupor that overshadowed the game.

- Urine samples taken from Bulgarian weightlifters **Anguel Guenchev** and **Mitko Grablev** showed the use of diuretics, and both were stripped of their gold medals at Seoul—days before Ben Johnson.

- **Lasse Viren**, winner of the 5,000 and 10,000 meter runs at the 1976 Olympics, was accused of blood doping, which enhances the oxygen supply. Though the practice was not considered illegal at the time, it was subsequently banned. Viren and other Finnish athletes eventually admitted to using blood doping, but were not subject to penalties.

Stanley Wilson

- Cuba's **Javier Sotomayor**, the only man to have high-jumped eight feet and one of the most popular athletes in the world, tested positive for cocaine at the 1999 Pan American Games.

- **Thomas "Hollywood" Henderson**, a Pro Bowl linebacker with the Dallas Cowboys, was cut in 1979 when he couldn't kick his drug habit. He was arrested in 1983 after smoking crack cocaine with two teenage girls, threatening them with a pistol, sexually assaulting one of them, and holding them against their will. He served twenty-eight months in jail.

Javier Sotomayor

- **Michelle Smith.** At the 1996 Summer Games, Smith came from obscurity to win three gold medals, making waves at the Olympic pool. Her competitors, in what was first thought to be sour grapes, wondered if she was clean. Their suspicions were proven correct two years later when Smith submitted to a random drug test at her home in Kilkenny. The sample was found to be contaminated with large amounts of alcohol, apparently whiskey. There was so much alcohol present that it would have been lethal had it been a legitimate sample. Based on this evidence, Smith was banned by swimming officials for four years; she retired in 1999. Her husband, Erik de Bruin, a Dutch discus thrower, had his career ended with his own four-year ban for using performance-enhancing drugs.

Michelle Smith

BASEBALL BUSTS

No sport has been more plagued by drug problems, or been more inept at dealing with them, than major league baseball.

Blame the players association, which virtually runs the sport. Blame the lack of a strong commissioner. Blame the leisure time available to rich athletes.

Steve Howe, a habitual drug abuser, was the first player to be suspended from baseball for life after pleading guilty to drug charges. The ban lasted five months.

Regardless of where you place the blame, the sagas of Steve Howe, Darryl Strawberry, and Dwight Gooden provide ample evidence of the trouble Major League Baseball has had with drug abusers.

Howe, the 1980 National League Rookie of the Year, was an outstanding left-handed reliever, a prized commodity in the majors. He was also a cocaine addict who, despite receiving repeated opportunities to change his ways, never got the message.

He was asked to clean up his act in 1982, when he underwent the first of many drug rehabilitations as a Los Angeles Dodger. His problems followed him to major-league stops in Minnesota and Texas and through a comeback bid in the minors. He was suspended a total of seven times.

Howe was arrested on December 19, 1991, while attempting to buy $100 worth of cocaine in Kalispell, Montana. After pleading guilty, he was suspended for life in 1992 by commissioner Fay Vincent—the first baseball player so sentenced.

The ban lasted all of five months as the union, on Howe's behalf, filed a grievance. Arbitrator George Nicolau ruled for Howe, trimming Howe's penalty to time served, saying the pitcher suffered from Attention Deficit Disorder.

Vincent's reaction summed up Howe's case and gave an indication of how helpless the sport had become when confronting drug abuse.

"It makes baseball look silly, and I think there'll be a lot of adverse reaction," said Vincent, who resigned as commissioner in the wake of Nicolau's ruling. "I don't think there was any doubt about my having just cause. I think the arbitrator substituted his judgment for mine, and the arbitrator was wrong . . . . I think it's a bad development for baseball. Why is eight different from seven?"

Howe actually made good on his final opportunity until being released by the Yankees on June 22, 1996. Two days later, he was arrested for carrying a loaded gun inside his luggage at a New York airport. Five months later, he pleaded guilty to gun possession and was placed on three years' probation and given 150 hours of community service.

A few months after that, he was charged with drunken driving in a motorcycle accident in which he suffered serious injuries. Charges were dropped when prosecutors decided that his blood test was obtained improperly.

And in 1999 he was banned from a volunteer coaching position with a girls' softball team because of his history of drug abuse. What the major leagues couldn't get straight a local organization could.

If anyone expected Major League Baseball to learn from Howe's seven suspensions, forget it. Just consider Strawberry's story. Or Gooden's.

In 1986, Gooden was twenty-one, possessed an intimidating fastball, and was headed for the Hall of Fame. Strawberry was twenty-four, could hit, field, run, and throw, and was also headed to Cooperstown. They both played for the world champion New York Mets.

The next year Gooden checked into the Smithers Center for treatment of cocaine addiction. Three years later, Strawberry was in the same facility for alcohol abuse.

Dwight Gooden, once a potential candidate for the Hall of Fame, was suspended for the entire 1995 season after failing two drug tests while serving an earlier suspension.

By 1994, both were in the midst of downward spirals that spoiled their reputations and jeopardized their careers. And, no, neither will be making any Hall of Fame speeches.

In 1994, Strawberry missed the first two and a half months of the season after admitting to a substance abuse problem. Just nine days after he left the Betty Ford Clinic, Gooden was suspended for sixty days after failing to follow his aftercare program for cocaine addiction. Gooden would then be banned for the entire 1995 season after failing two drug tests while serving the earlier suspension.

Not to be outdone, Strawberry has been given three substance-abuse suspensions, including one for the entire 2000 season. After being indicted for tax evasion and for not making child support payments, he was ordered to repay $350,000 in back taxes and sentenced to six months of home confinement.

In March 2000, a few weeks before he was to host a fundraiser at the Southside Boys & Girls Club in St. Petersburg, Florida, Strawberry again tested positive for drug use. Ironically, the fundraiser was for youth drug prevention programs.

New York Yankee Darryl Strawberry could hit, field, run, and throw. But he could not beat a drug addiction.

Kevin Campbell (left) and Jim Varao, both of Tampa, Florida hold a sign during spring season in protest of New York Yankees outfielder Darryl Strawberry's drug use. Strawberry, who tested positive for cocaine, worked out with his teammates, then was ordered off the field by baseball while it investigated his failed drug test.

REVERSE ROBIN HOODS

A lawyer-agent cheats his hockey-playing clients, even as he is bettering their working environment. A promoter takes millions from his boxers, even as he is filling their pockets with thousands. A trainer thinks nothing of cheating to guarantee his fighter's success, regardless of the repercussions. A ballplayer engages in racketeering, extortion, fraud, and conspiracy.

And they call the sports world Fun and Games.

Not as far as Alan Eagleson, Don King, Panama Lewis, and Denny McLain are concerned. They all crossed the line, as their shocking stories will show.

Alan Eagleson once controlled a sport, the most powerful man in hockey.

Denny McLain once dominated a sport, the best pitcher in baseball.

Years later, they were both serving time in federal prison for criminal activities.

While there have been many athletes through the decades who have committed crimes and served time, the stories of Eagleson and McLain perfectly exemplify how power, greed, poor judgment, or simply associating with the wrong people can lead to a humiliating downfall.

The ancient Greeks didn't play hockey or baseball, but they would have understood—and been fascinated by—the tragedies of Eagleson and McLain.

Eagleson latched onto the coattails of Bobby Orr, the Boston Bruins defenseman who changed the way the game of hockey was played with his speed, daring, and ingenuity. In 1966, Orr was the first hockey star to hire an agent, Eagleson.

Soon Eagleson had an impressive stable of 200 clients, and not only was he negotiating contracts for the players but his assistants were

Alan Eagleson, former executive director of the NHL Players Association, once considered running for Prime Minister of Canada. In the meantime, he was ripping off disability insurance money, overcharging players as their union boss, and pocketing huge sums meant for their pension funds.

Chicago Blackhawk Tony Esposito
met with Eagleson as the players
representative in talks regarding a
collective bargaining agreement.

handling promotional appearances and
endorsement opportunities as well. Thanks
greatly to Eagleson, NHL players who, as late
as the end of the 1960s, were holding second
jobs could now live comfortably off their
hockey salaries and ancillary earnings.

As executive director of the NHL Players
Association, Eagleson became the main power-
broker in the sport, more influential than NHL
president Clarence Campbell and his successor,

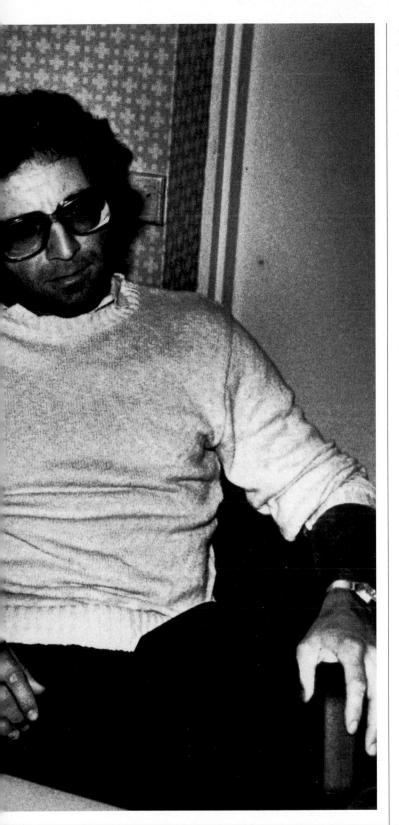

John Ziegler. He even talked of running for prime minister of Canada some day.

Supposedly, Eagleson's greatest contribution to the players, his legacy, would be the formation of international events such as the USSR-Canada Summit Series in 1972—the first meeting between the superpowers of hockey—and the Canada Cup. While the players basically skated for nothing, donating their time in late summer to represent their countries, their pension fund coffers were overflowing like Niagara Falls.

Supposedly.

First, Eagleson began strong-arming sponsors of the international events he ran. He told Labatt Brewing Company, whose slogans adorned the sideboards during the 1984 Canada Cup, that all advertising revenue for the tournament belonged to the International Ice Hockey Federation. That was a blatant lie, yet uninformed Labatt yielded and a half-million dollars wound up in Eagleson's control.

Amazingly, when Labatt sponsored the 1991 tournament, it hired Eagleson to negotiate the non-existent advertising rights with the IIHF—meaning that Labatt paid Eagleson for doing nothing. Twice.

But those scams paled compared to how he cheated the players he represented. Orr was essentially broke when he severed relations with Eagleson in 1980. Although Orr had earned several million dollars, Eagleson had either mishandled it or, worse, taken it.

When other players challenged Eagleson about how he came to acquire his multifaceted empire, or about how their money was being invested, they got nowhere fast.

"In those days, most of the guys had a huge passion to play, but they hadn't finished high school," said Hall of Fame defenseman Brad Park and former vice president of the NHLPA. "When they'd get up to ask him a question he didn't like, he'd tear them a new rear end. That shut a lot of people up."

Fortunately, they didn't remain quiet for long. Instead, they hired private investigators and auditors, who discovered a pattern of deceit by Eagleson. He was ripping off their disability insurance money. He was overcharging players as their union boss. He was pocketing huge sums meant for their pension fund.

Carl Brewer, who helped found the NHLPA that Eagleson would oversee, spent nearly twenty-five years searching for the money Eagleson took from the pension fund. At Eagleson's sentencing, one of hockey's toughest players broke down and cried.

Perhaps he was weeping because Eagleson was given an eighteen-month sentence, thanks to a plea bargain, and would serve only six months in a minimum security prison. Or that he was fined only $1 million, a small portion of what he embezzled, for being found guilty on three counts of mail fraud in the United States and three more in Canada.

Or maybe there was some joy in those tears: Eagleson, once among the most powerful men in sports, was disbarred as a lawyer, stripped of his Order of Canada, and forced to resign from the Hockey Hall of Fame after Bobby Orr, Gordie Howe, and sixteen other greats said they would drop out if Eagleson stayed in.

Denny McLain once appeared headed for the Baseball Hall of Fame.

Just when Orr was at his peak, McLain was untouchable on the mound. In 1968, he won thirty-one games, leading the Detroit Tigers to the World Series title. He was the first pitcher in thirty-four years to win thirty games—and nobody has done it since.

McLain wasn't just a hero in Detroit, he was lauded throughout baseball for his tenacity, durability, and, of course, the masterful way he handled hitters.

Only he didn't handle his business affairs nearly so well.

Two years after a season that should have catapulted the hard-throwing right-hander to the Hall of Fame, McLain was suspended by commissioner Bowie Kuhn for "involvement in 1967 bookmaking activities and his associations

at that time. McLain's association in 1967 with gamblers was contrary to his obligation as a professional baseball player to conform to high standards of personal conduct," said Kuhn.

McLain returned midway through the schedule, but was suspended again on September 9, 1970, for violating terms of his baseball probation.

Just two years after that, McLain retired at the age of twenty-eight with a 131-91 lifetime record.

Soon McLain fell into a pattern of illegal betting and bookmaking, eventually becoming part of a loanshark scheme. Federal authorities claimed he threatened violence to collect debts for which he charged usurious rates of up to 150 percent.

Charged with racketeering, conspiracy, and extortion, as well as drug possession, McLain was found guilty in 1985. On April 26, U.S. District Judge Elizabeth Kovachevich admonished McLain for "failure to admit to yourself your own guilt." She then sentenced him to twenty-three years, including the maximum of fifteen years for trying to deal three kilos of cocaine in 1982.

"I've brought enormous shame on my entire family," he said.

McLain also claimed to be "dead broke" and unable to file an appeal. He said his wife and four children had to borrow money and sell two cars for less than $1,500 to keep out of debt.

But lawyers filed an appeal anyway—and won.

The 11th U.S. Circuit Court of Appeals overturned the conviction in August 1987, criticizing Kovachevich's handling of the four-month trial. McLain served twenty-nine months of his sentence at a federal prison in Alabama.

When the autobiography he wrote in prison, *Strikeout: The Story of Denny McLain*, was published by *The Sporting News*, his future appeared bright.

"You really quickly learn what you've lost and really come to know how much life can be abused and how much maybe you've abused it in the past," McLain said. "I don't intend on abusing any of it anymore."

A few months later, he pleaded guilty to federal racketeering and drug charges in an agreement he made to avoid another trial. When he was sentenced to time already served and five years of probation, McLain termed it "an early Christmas present."

But it wasn't long before McLain turned into the Grinch.

In 1993, McLain and several associates purchased the Peet Packing Company, the largest employer in Chesaning, Michigan. A mere

Mickey Lolich, a teammate of McLain's, said, "We used to say he was either going to wind up in concrete shoes or in prison. I guess he got the latter."

eighteen months later, the plant was forced to close, with all 200 employees losing their jobs.

Investigators quickly began looking at the company's pension fund, and soon accused McLain and Roger Smigiel of stealing more than three million from the fund.

They looked in the right place. McLain was convicted and sentenced to eight years in prison, while Smigiel was given seven years. They were ordered to repay $2.5 million.

Not that the victimized families could take much solace.

"It doesn't bring back the company and the jobs," said Wallace H. Peet, great-grandson of the 109-year-old company's founder. "A lot of people are still hurting financially because of their recklessness with the pension fund. I'm glad their sentences are fairly stiff, but they weren't prosecuted for putting the company out of business."

"Maybe it would be different if something positive could come out of it, but jail time doesn't help us any," added Robert Ptacek, who had worked twenty-one years at Peet. "He took away the future for our families."

While serving the embezzlement sentence, McLain was indicted on federal charges that he took part in a scheme involving fraudulent phone cards. The government dropped the case for lack of evidence.

Mickey Lolich, the other star pitcher with the Tigers in the 1960s, wasn't surprised about his former teammate's problems.

"He was always in trouble all his life," Lolich said. "We used to say he was either going to wind up in concrete shoes or in prison. I guess he got the latter."

From pitching balls to pitching deals, Denny McLain's lifetime achievements of racketeering, conspiracy, and extortion overshadowed his career with the Detroit Tigers.

PANAMA LEWIS

In the 1970s, Carlos "Panama" Lewis was a rising force among boxing cornermen. He worked with Ray Arcel, one of the sport's greatest trainers, and was part of Roberto Duran's team. And, later, Mike Tyson's.

Lewis was in Aaron Pryor's corner for his all-out war against Alexis Arguello for the junior welterweight title in November 1982. Pryor was reeling as he returned to his corner after the thirteenth round.

Ringside microphones picked up Lewis' voice ordering that Pryor be given "the special bottle" to drink from, "the one I mixed myself." A rejuvenated Pryor knocked out Arguello in the next round. Boxing officials never could locate that special bottle.

That was child's play compared to what Lewis was involved in the following summer.

Luis Resto, a mediocre middleweight, was in with Billy Collins, an undefeated hotshot with designs on the title. The bout was on the June 16, 1983, undercard of Duran's WBA junior middleweight title fight with Davey Moore, a highly publicized match.

Resto-Collins was supposed to be nothing more than a warmup event—until Resto, with a record of 20-7-2, pummeled Collins.

"It feels like he's got rocks in his gloves," said Collins once he returned to his corner.

Collins suffered fractures of the orbital bones surrounding both eyes. His vision never would return to normal.

He also sustained severe psychological damage from the beating. Collins would never box again. He became an alcoholic and, one night, was killed in an auto accident, leaving behind an infant daughter and claims by his father that Billy committed suicide.

Fighters get beaten up badly in the ring all the time, but this case was different. Lewis had removed the horse-hair padding from Resto's gloves. He might as well have handed Resto a battering ram.

"You don't think Resto knew he didn't have padding in the gloves?" said Collins' father, Billy Ray Collins. "You don't think Panama Lewis took it out? They killed him. They killed my son."

Both Lewis and Resto were convicted of assault, conspiracy, and tampering with the outcome of a sporting event. They were banned from boxing for life and Lewis served just under three years of a six-year prison sentence.

To this day, Lewis claims he was innocent of shaving the padding from Resto's gloves.

"I was a scapegoat," he said, blaming Resto's cutman, the late Artie Curley. "I was in charge of the corner, but I didn't do it. I'm sorry for the part I played in the event, but if Artie Curley was still alive, I wouldn't be involved in all of this. He put the gloves on Resto."

Lewis also claimed that Arcel instructed him to get rid of the gloves before the boxing commission could seize them. Resto, however, knows who is to blame.

"That whole thing makes me angry," Resto said. "Panama, he can go to hell."

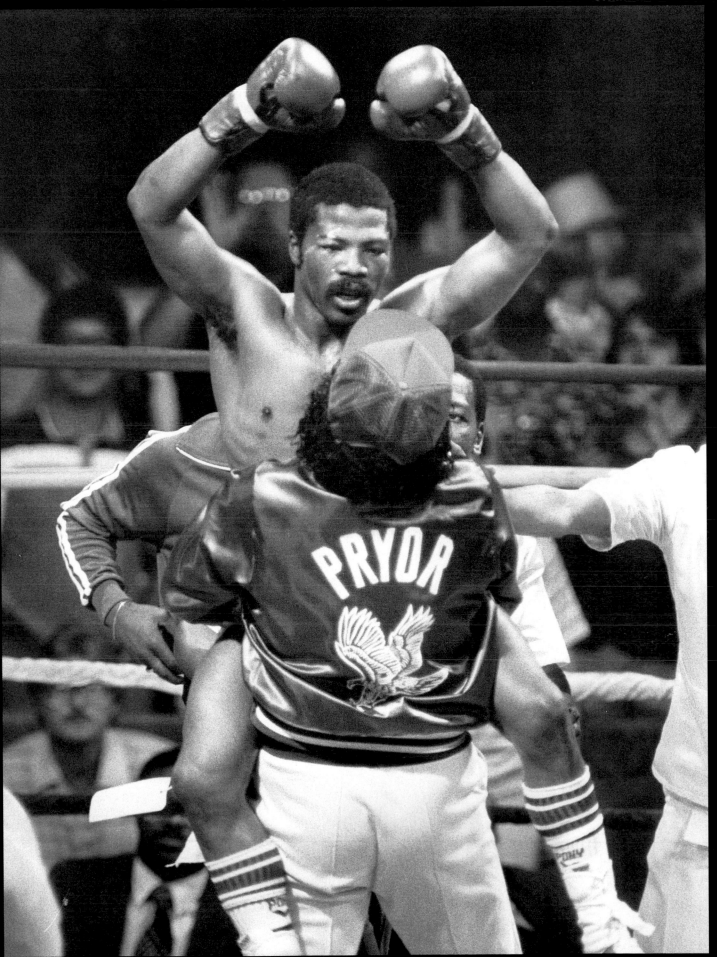

DON KING

The self-proclaimed "world's greatest promoter" and the man who brought eight-figure payoffs to boxing, shot and killed a man trying to rob one of his gambling operations in 1954. He was cleared after claiming self-defense, but, thirteen years later, was convicted of second-degree murder for stomping to death numbers runner Samuel Garrett over a $600 debt.

King was sentenced to life in prison. A judge later reduced the conviction to manslaughter and King was paroled in 1971, then pardoned two years later by Ohio Governor James Rhodes.

Don King and Mike Tyson's professional relationship was worthy of the boxing ring. Verbal punches and accusations were exchanged even when Tyson was in prison.

Since then, he has escaped conviction for embezzling, tax evasion, and for filing a bogus insurance claim. He has been the subject of three grand jury investigations and an FBI sting operation. Yet when he has been brought to trial, King's defense attorneys have gotten him off or benefitted from hung juries.

One juror in a 1999 trial involving a dispute over rematch rights for boxer Miguel Angel Gonzalez said, "Once you take away the hot air and the verbiage, I'd never want to draw up a contract with him."

King's most grievous missteps have come in his dealings with the very same fighters he has enriched by bringing huge prize money into boxing. While he was greatly responsible for making multimillionaires out of Larry Holmes, Julio Cesar Chavez, and dozens of other champions, he also duped many of them out of money they rightfully earned in the ring.

King usually claimed the funds went to various expenses that were taken out of boxers' purses. But then, somehow, that money wound up in the coffers of King Enterprises.

He has been accused of fixing the rankings by offering sanctioning bodies payoffs to advance his fighters. One rival promoter remarked that King and World Boxing Council president Jose Sulaiman "are in bed together so often they share the same pillow and blanket."

King's reply?

"I'm a promoter," King says. "I am representing law and order, because without law and order you have nothing. You have chaos."

Actually, King is good at chaos, too. When Chavez, Mexico's biggest sports hero of the last twenty years, tried to hire another promoter while under contract to King—this is boxing, of course, where contracts rarely are honored—King went to a full-court press. By bringing legal action, he successfully placed Chavez's career in limbo before a Florida appeals court ruled that King couldn't block Chavez from fighting. In the meantime, Chavez missed out on several lucrative offers.

No fighter prospered more from a relationship with King than Mike Tyson. And no boxer suffered more from that association.

Tyson's life changed for the better, and then for the worse, during his relationship with King. Before he

Jose Sulaiman, (left) President of the World Boxing Congress, celebrates twenty years as the organization's president with boxing promoter Don King, (right) in Mexico City. Absent was longtime King fighter Julio Cesar Chavez, who testified against King in a 1995 trial in New York.

became heavyweight champion, Tyson fought every month or so. The anger pent up inside of him was released on his unfortunate opponents, and Tyson walked the straight and narrow.

But once he reached the top and fought just a few times a year, Tyson fell off the edge socially and began to run into trouble with the law. He couldn't release his anger in the ring, so he got into trouble outside of it.

His promoter and confidant during those most difficult times was Don King.

Guilt by association? Perhaps. Tyson filed a $100 million lawsuit in 1998 against King, claiming that much in lost or misplaced earnings.

Even King's most loyal (some would say "most duped") subject eventually turned on him.

"King knew that Tyson had a fundamental inability to read and understand contracts and fully appreciate the effect of business transactions on his life," it said in the lawsuit filed in U.S. District Court in New York.

The suit also suggested that King broke laws in Florida, Nevada, and Pennsylvania through secret deals that allowed him to pocket higher percentages of fight purses than he was contracted to receive. Tyson claimed he lost $45 million between 1995 and 1997 alone.

Tyson also accused King of visiting him in prison and persuading him to sign contracts when he knew Tyson had no access to an attorney.

King's reply?

"I just feel deeply hurt and saddened that Mike Tyson would allow himself to be used as a pawn and manipulated," King said. "He knows that I treated him fairly."

In boxing, all is fair in love and war—as long as you hurt everyone but yourself.

Like a cat with nine lives, boxing promoter Don King is found innocent yet again on July 9, 1998, after charges were filed that he faked a contract. In 1971 he was paroled from prison when a second-degree murder charge was reduced to manslaughter. He was pardoned two years later by Ohio governor James Rhodes.

CRIMINALS LIST

• **J.T. LUNDY.** Calumet Farms once was the pride of Kentucky, the place where champions were bred. As president of Calumet, Lundy ran the farm into the ground, and the Lexington, Kentucky, stables declared bankruptcy in 1991. A year later, it was sold at auction for $17 million.

Government investigators soon discovered that Lundy and Gary Matthews, the farm's finance administrator, had bribed a bank official to secure a $65 million loan. And one of Calumet's greatest horses, Alydar, was euthanized following a mysterious accident in which the horse broke his leg. Calumet cashed in a $35 million insurance policy on the stallion.

Lundy and Matthews were convicted of conspiracy, fraud, and bribery.

● **GRAHAM JAMES.** How scary is it to think that an adult who is teaching children to play sports is also sexually abusing the youngsters?

Graham James, coach of the Western Hockey League's Swift Current Broncos, was sentenced to forty-two months in prison in 1987 after former NHL player Sheldon Kennedy revealed the abuse. James pleaded guilty to committing dozens of sexual assaults on Kennedy and an unidentified player in the most embarrassing and highly publicized scandal ever to hit Canadian youth hockey.

Allen Iverson sits inside a courtroom before the start of his preliminary hearing in New Kent, Virigina. The 1997 NBA rookie of the year pleaded no contest to carrying a concealed weapon, but had a drug charge dismissed.

● **ALLEN IVERSON.** Years before becoming the top pick in the NBA draft and then a pro all-star, Iverson was a jailbird.

In February 1993, Iverson was arrested and charged with maiming by mob for his role in a Hampton, Virginia, bowling alley brawl that reportedly was racially motivated. He was convicted on three counts and sentenced to five years in prison, but served only four months before he was granted conditional clemency by Governor L. Douglas Wilder and released from a prison farm.

The Virginia Court of Appeals reversed Iverson's conviction two years later. But two years after that Iverson was arrested and charged with drug and firearms possession after the car in which he was riding was stopped for speeding. He pleaded no contest to a misdemeanor firearms charge; the drug charge was dropped. Under a plea bargain, Iverson was placed on three years probation.

NEGATIVE

NEWSMAKERS

TONYA, O.J., AND LATRELL

They're bad news. They made headlines and drew high television ratings for all the wrong reasons. From the Tonya and Nancy saga to the O.J. Trial, from Latrell Sprewell's attack on his coach to John Rocker's big mouth to Dennis Rodman's, well, everything — these are the worst offenders of the fair play and role model sports doctrine.

So turn the pages and don't be shocked by what you read.

A Hall of Fame football player and national champion figure skater wouldn't seem to have much in common. But in 1994, they dominated the headlines.

While O.J. Simpson and Tonya Harding never were convicted of any crimes or served any time, their perceived villainy made for two of the most mesmerizing sagas of recent times. Add in Latrell Sprewell's physical attack on his coach and you've got three circumstances unmatched among athletes who never wound up in jail.

Harding wasn't a typical personality in the elegant world of figure skating. She shot pool, drove around in a pickup truck, and smoked cigarettes. But she could jump through the roof, and that helped her rise through the ranks of a

sport where glamour and glitz usually reign.

By the 1994 U.S. championships, which also served as the Olympic trials for the Lillehammer Games, Harding had won a national title, a world silver medal, and finished fourth at the 1992 Olympics. She was one of only two women—and the only American—to successfully perform the difficult triple axel jump in competition.

She believed the Lillehammer gold was in reach. Her husband, Jeff Gillooly, thought so too, and he hatched a plan to ensure that Harding would earn one of the two spots on the U.S. team.

Unfortunately for Harding, Gillooly and his cohorts made the Three Stooges look like geniuses. Their inept attempt to eliminate Nancy Kerrigan as a challenger would have been

American figure skater Tonya Harding tries to rev up the crowd as she leaves the ice after a practice session in Hamar, Norway.

comical had it not been so mean-spirited.

Gillooly hired longtime friend Shawn Eckardt, Shane Stant, and Stant's uncle, Derrick Smith, to arrange an attack on Kerrigan that would sideline her for the Olympics. Eckardt, a huge, hulking man whom his sentencing judge later would call "infamous, notorious, greedy, dishonest, even stupid," believed he would be hired by world-class skaters to protect them after they saw what happened to Kerrigan. The rest of the incompetent quartet figured they would get rich off Harding's success once Kerrigan was out of the way.

Stant was the hit man. On January 6 in Detroit's Cobo Hall—next door to the site of the competition, Joe Louis Arena—Kerrigan was leaving the ice after a practice session. As she stepped off, a masked man slammed her just above the right knee with a police baton. Two inches lower and he would have likely ended Kerrigan's career.

As he fled, Kerrigan screamed in agony, "Why? Why?"

Stant ran through a plexiglass window and into the street, where Smith was waiting in the getaway car. Mission accomplished.

Kerrigan withdrew from nationals, which Harding won. Both were selected for the Olympic team as pundits jokingly wondered where Harding was during the attack.

Already, however, investigators were uncovering signs that Gillooly might have been involved. Quickly, more and more evidence was discovered linking him and, eventually, the other three men, to the crime. Eckardt even told a minister about the plot.

Meanwhile, the Tonya-Nancy saga had become fodder for the evening news and headline

The ending to the Harding-Kerrigan soap opera was TV perfect: Harding blew her performance and Kerrigan won a silver medal at the 1994 Winter Olympic Games.

material for the tabloids. Hundreds of media members descended on Portland, Oregon. Harding's hometown. And the questions on everyone's lips: Did Tonya know? If so, when? And did she plan the whole thing?

Harding steadfastly denied any knowledge or guilt. But when Harding was interviewed for ten hours at FBI headquarters two weeks after the attack, she changed her story and implicated Gillooly, with whom she had split. Gillooly, in turn, claimed Harding planned the whole thing, even as Harding was saying her life was threatened by Gillooly if she didn't go along with the plot.

"I learned that some persons that were close to me may have been involved in the assault. My first reaction was one of disbelief, and the disbelief was followed by shock and fear," she said. "I still want to represent my country in Lillehammer. Despite my mistakes and my rough edges, I have nothing—I have done nothing to violate the standards of excellence, of sportsmanship that are expected in an Olympic athlete . . . .

"I have devoted my entire life to one objective: winning an Olympic gold medal for my country. This is my last chance. I ask only for your understanding and the opportunity to represent my country with the best figure skating performance of my life."

Kerrigan, meanwhile, recovered quickly and made the trip to Lillehammer. She admitted to being "shocked" upon learning that Harding might have been involved in the scheme.

But the real shock might have been the helplessness of U.S. Olympic officials. Rather than risk losing a $25 million damage lawsuit filed by Harding, the USOC cancelled a hearing that could have led to her being dismissed from the team and allowed Tonya to skate in Lillehammer.

Tonya Harding shows her skate to the judges after interruputing her free skating program at the 1994 Winter Olympics.

This soap opera had so galvanized America that the first practice session in which Harding and Kerrigan skated together was televised live—a first. The short program drew the kind of ratings only the Super Bowl can match. So did the free skate, from which Harding—already hopelessly out of the medals competition after a poor opening routine—almost withdrew.

Facing disqualification, Harding appeared to perform her program with just seconds remaining before the grace period expired. She blew her opening jump, then stopped skating forty-five seconds into the routine and, crying, went directly to the referee to show him a broken shoelace. Her performance was postponed for nearly a half hour, but even so she failed to distinguish herself when she returned to the ice.

"I think I did quite well under the circumstances," she said, "because I think I was ready to have a nervous breakdown before I went out the first time."

Kerrigan, who certainly could have been excused for a case of nerves, skated brilliantly to win a silver medal behind Oksana Baiul.

The on-ice confrontation was over—Tonya and Nancy never spoke and barely exchanged glances—but Harding's strange story continued. She served three years probation after pleading guilty to conspiracy to hinder prosecution. Harding also was ordered to pay $160,000 in fines and fees and perform 500 hours of community service.

Gillooly pleaded guilty to racketeering and was sentenced to two years in prison and fined $100,000.

Eckardt, Stant, and Smith all were sentenced to eighteen months in prison.

Worst of all for the would-be ice queen, Harding was banned from competition for life by the U.S. Figure Skating Association.

Just as the Tonya-Nancy scandal was ebbing, along came another headline-grabbing, TV ratings bonanza of yet another sordid story: the grizzly murders of Nicole Brown Simpson, former wife of O.J. Simpson, and her friend Ron Goldman. They were found with their throats slashed outside Nicole Simpson's condo.

Almost immediately, investigators focused on Simpson as a suspect. And when he attempted a getaway, nearly every American watched breathlessly. And when he was acquitted, nearly every American expressed an opinion on the verdict.

Simpson was one of the greatest running backs in college history, winning the 1968 Heisman Trophy and leading Southern Cal to a national title. He then played for the Buffalo Bills of the NFL, becoming the first man to rush for 2,000 yards in a season.

After his playing days Simpson became a celebrity, first as an announcer on *Monday Night Football* then as an actor.

But there was a darker side to Simpson which came to light after the murders on June 12, 1994. Nicole had previously called police to complain about being assaulted by her husband, whose temper tantrums in public were well-publicized; grand jury transcripts would depict Simpson as a jealous man who stalked his ex-wife.

On June 13 Simpson flew to Chicago, where he was told about the murders. Even as he was heading back to Los Angeles, detectives were conducting a search of his estate—without a warrant.

Three days later, he accompanied his children Sydney and Justin to Nicole's funeral, unaware that the police were about to accuse him of killing her and Goldman.

The next day, Simpson was charged and his lawyer agreed to Simpson's surrender. But Simpson and another former pro football player, Al Cowlings, climbed into Simpson's white Ford Bronco and began driving along the California freeways.

As police were hunting for Simpson, threatening to prosecute anybody who helped the fugitive, the Bronco was sighted. Inside, Simpson held a gun to his head as Cowlings drove.

Media helicopters equipped with television

This was the face of a Hollywood celebrity. Football player, announcer,
and actor, Simpson was getting coverage like he never had before,
only this time for accusations of a double-murder.

cameras soon took up the sixty-mile slow-motion chase, following the Bronco's progress as police cars followed at a distance. Pedestrians ran to the shoulder of the highway and waved, cheering Simpson in a surreal scene that, appropriately, took place in the shadow of the Hollywood hills. Millions watched on television as regular programming was pre-empted.

Amid claims by his supporters that Simpson was disoriented and not, therefore, attempting an escape, he finally surrendered at his Brentwood home. Cowlings was also arrested, but was later released for lack of evidence.

"The slowness of this chase makes it hard for

people to treat this as a deliberate flight from justice," said UCLA law professor Peter Arenella.

The ensuing trial was as riveting as one of Simpson's broken-field runs. His flamboyant attorney, Johnnie Cochran, Jr., and prosecutors Marcia Clark and Christopher Darden became fixtures on the evening news. At times, testimony

by such witnesses as Brian "Kato" Kaelin, Simpson's houseboy, and detective Mark Fuhrman—whom the defense team claimed had planted evidence—overshadowed Simpson.

So did the sometimes engimatic proclamations from Judge Lance Ito, who also became a media darling during the trial.

The trial and its accompanying media frenzy lasted from the first witness' testimony on January 31, 1995 until the jury deliberated a mere four hours before returning the not guilty verdict on October 3.

O.J. Simpson was a free man.

And a social pariah, shunned by the people who flocked around him before the murder case.

When two No. 32 football jerseys and a Pro Football Hall of Fame induction certificate were set ablaze and two trophies were smashed outside the LA Criminal Courts Building, protest organizer Bob Enyart said:

"We are destroying O.J. Simpson's property in front of the LA courthouse because the criminal justice system is destroying justice before our very eyes."

Simpson would later be found liable by a civil jury for the deaths of his ex-wife and her friend and was assessed a $33.5 million judgment.

In attempting to pay off his debts, Simpson held an auction at which, for a $255,500 price tag, his Heisman Trophy was sold.

Five years after the deaths, Simpson viewed himself as a victim.

"Everyone used this as their cause, and I've learned to live with it," Simpson said. "It isn't about me anymore. It's about having a scapegoat."

Murder defendant O.J. Simpson grimaces as he tries on one of the leather gloves prosecutors say he wore the night his ex-wife Nicole Brown Simpson and Ron Goldman were murdered.

While there were no witnesses to point a finger at Simpson, and Harding allegedly hired someone else to do the swinging, there is no contesting Sprewell's villainous act.

As a member of the Golden State Warriors, the long-range bomber did some close-in handiwork on his coach, P.J. Carlesimo. On December 1, 1997, Sprewell put both his hands around Carlesimo's neck and choked him.

Warriors assistant coaches immediately jumped in to break it up, but Carlesimo already had thick scratches on his neck—and the NBA had itself a scandal.

"We aren't going to tolerate the conduct that was displayed on the court today," Warriors GM Garry St. Jean said after Sprewell not only choked Carlesimo but, fifteen minutes later, returned to the practice gym to confront the coach again, only to be held back by teammates.

The team meted out a swift suspension of ten games, but then NBA commissioner David Stern, sensing the gravity of such an incident, extended the suspension for the rest of the season.

"A sports league does not have to accept or condone behavior that would not be tolerated in any other segment of society," Stern said.

Sprewell never has shown any real contrition for the episode; there have been several carefully worded apologies, however. Sprewell insists he wasn't trying to hurt Carlesimo, just make him stop riding him so hard.

At one point, in describing the incident, Sprewell tried this spin:

"I wasn't choking P.J., I mean, P.J., he could breathe. It's not like he was losing air or anything like that. I mean, it wasn't a choke, I wasn't trying to kill P.J. If you're choking someone, you don't get scratches. You get welts totally around your neck. It's not like I was going to sit there and kill the man. No, I would have stopped, definitely.

"It was all about the respect factor with me. It was all about P.J. disrespecting me as a man. You don't talk to people the way that P.J. talked to me. To have my pride and my respect and my manhood means more than any dollar amount."

But claiming he was a victim of racial descrimination when the league banned him for the remainder of a year—costing him $24 million—Sprewell turned around and sued the league and the team for $30 million. After the case was dismissed by a federal judge, he filed another lawsuit, claiming NBA security officials destroyed evidence that could have exonerated him.

"People think I'm almost like a maniac on the court," he said. "People have this perception of me as an evil person, a bad person. People look at me now like I'm the symbol for the bad boy of the NBA."

Carlesimo never filed charges, and, in an odd juxtaposition, Sprewell wound up profiting while the coach was fired two seasons later.

First, arbitrator John Feerick ruled that the contract termination and suspension were excessive. He ordered that Sprewell be reinstated by the Warriors and that the suspension end July 1, not December 1, 1998.

Sprewell suggested the Warriors fire Carlesimo and bring him back.

"My problem is with P.J." Sprewell said. "I hope the Warriors make some kind of change or they're not going to be very good in the future."

Sprewell's future would include a trade to New York, where he earned $9 million and the adoration of Knicks fans, who immediately forgot his attack on Carlesimo when Spree threw down a three. He also would ink a five-year, $61.8 million contract extension in 1999.

" ... People look at me now like I'm the symbol for the bad boy of the NBA," said Sprewell after the choking incident. The NBA suspended Sprewell for the season and Sprewell sued the league and the team, claiming he was a victim of racial discrimination.

Golden State Warriors head coach P.J. Carlesimo appears with welts on his neck during a news conference announcing the suspension of guard Latrell Sprewell. Carlesimo was physically assaulted by Sprewell during team practice, resulting in a ten-game suspension by the Warriors.

And his future after the confrontation with Carlesimo would include suing his agent for failing to negotiate a salary protection clause in his contract with the Warriors; pleading no contest to a reckless driving charge, for which he was sentenced to three months of home detention—witnesses said he was speeding and weaving in traffic; suing Converse after the shoe company terminated his endorsement contract; and receiving a fine of $10,000 by the NBA for profane and vulgar remarks to taunting fans in his first game back in Oakland.

Sprewell also snubbed Carlesimo when the coach offered to shake hands before the Warriors' visit to Madison Square Garden.

To his credit, Sprewell didn't gloat when Carlesimo was fired on December 29, 1999.

"The way our league is, players and coaches are often given second and third opportunities to play and coach at other places," Sprewell said. "I would expect he would show up somewhere."

Hopefully, not at a practice attended by Sprewell.

"I wasn't choking P.J., I mean, P.J., he could breathe. It's not like he was losing air or anything..." said Latrell Sprewell in defense of accusations that he tried to strangle Golden State coach P.J. Carlesimo.

OFF HIS ROCKER

John Rocker can throw a baseball 100 mph. He can ignore the stress of having the bases loaded when he enters a game. He performs very well one of the most difficult jobs in all of sports: major league relief pitcher.

Too bad he can't keep his mouth shut.

Rocker claims he isn't a racist or a bigot. But he doesn't deny making the following comments to *Sports Illustrated* in 1999:

"Imagine having to take the #7 train to [Shea Stadium] looking like you're [in] Beirut next to some kid with purple hair, next to some queer with AIDS, right next to some dude who got out of jail for the fourth time, right next to some 20-year-old mom with four kids. It's depressing.

"The biggest thing I don't like about New York are the foreigners. You can walk an entire block in Times Square and not hear anybody speaking English. Asians and Koreans and Vietnamese and Indians and Russians and Spanish people and everything up there. How the hell did they get in this country?"

And how the hell did Rocker not get more than a slap on the wrist from Major League Baseball and his team, the Atlanta Braves, for making such idiotic comments?

Simple. The baseball players' union basically runs the sport. So, when Rocker was suspended until May 1 by commissioner Bud Selig and fined $20,000, the left-hander appealed—with the backing of the union. Naturally, he won, and arbitrator Shyam Das reduced the sentence by two months and the fine to a laughable $500.

Even worse, Rocker received standing ovations during spring training and in his first appearance in Atlanta for the Braves, following his suspension.

Right-thinking people were offended by the hero-worship accorded to the latest Mouth of the South.

Presidential candidates Al Gore, Bill Bradley, and George W. Bush [former owner of the Texas Rangers] criticized Rocker.

"I don't know John Rocker, and I don't want to know John Rocker," said Bradley, a former pro basketball star.

Added Gore: "I, first of all, think what he said was reprehensible and disgusting. And I condemn it without any reservation, of course."

And Bush: "In athletics, this is a world of some young men who make a lot of money who . . . who aren't responsible for their behavior."

Hall of Famer Hank Aaron, the greatest of all Braves players, was outraged by Rocker's statements, even suggesting that the team for which "Hammering Hank" still worked should consider dumping the pitcher.

"I am very sick and disgusted about the whole situation. I

John Rocker stirred up a lot of emotions with racist remarks made during an interview with *Sports Illustrated*.

Atlanta Braves pitcher John Rocker is shown, in New York in this October 17, 1999, photo. Rocker admitted to ESPN on January 12, 2000, that his racial and ethnic comments in a magazine article made him sound like a "complete jerk."

have no place in my heart for people who feel that way," Aaron said. After a meeting with Rocker that also included former U.N. ambassador and Atlanta mayor Andrew Young, Aaron encouraged the pitcher to get counseling.

"He is a good pitcher, but he has got to learn to be a celebrity," said Young.

Celebrities who were outraged included the rock band Twisted Sister, whose "I Wanna Rock" was played by the Braves whenever Rocker entered a game. The group asked the team to stop using their song for Rocker.

"We've got Hispanics in this band, Italians in this band, people who are Polish and Russian," said guitarist Jay Jay French, the band's co-founder. "We're all immigrants, all 'foreigners,' and this is our way of saying his comments were not acceptable."

Rocker, who also referred to a teammate as a "fat monkey," was contrite about his remarks. Naturally, he denied they were a true indication of how he felt.

"Even though it might appear otherwise from what I've said, I am not a racist," Rocker said. "I should not have said what I did because it is not what I believe in my heart."

Convincing anyone of that is another story.

BASKETBALL'S BAD BOY

When Dennis Rodman signed with the Dallas Mavericks in the middle of the 1999–2000 NBA season, it set up a perfect punch line for comedians: Now the Mavericks had the Ultimate Maverick.

A maverick at times in a blond wig, heavy makeup, and lipstick who can pluck a basketball off a backboard as well as pluck his eyebrows. Rodman thinks nothing of flaunting his rebellious, anti-social behavior in society's face: head-butting a team mascot, kicking a cameraman, and deliberately hitting an opposing player in the groin. And the beat goes on.

A disruptive influence on the Mavericks? Team owner Mark Cuban wasn't concerned, figuring Rodman's rebounding skills would overshadow his reputation as the Bad Boy of Basketball.

"I'm not going to try to stop Dennis from being Dennis," Cuban said. "I'm not going to say, 'Oooh, Dennis, don't go and party. Oooh, Dennis, you're talking to the wrong girls.' No, Dennis, go out and have fun—be Dennis."

To some players around the league, that was just the problem. As Phoenix Suns guard Jason Kidd said, "There are players who have red flags next to their names." In Rodman's case, it's red, white, and blue hair—or, depending upon his mood, lemon-lime or chartreuse. Anything to be noticed.

Eventually, Cuban's patience would be put to the test as The Dennis the Menace Show swung into high gear. Despite promises that he had changed for the better, the "Worm" had suddenly turned back into his Evil Twin. Soon Rodman had worn out his welcome—again. This time he lasted only twelve games, the shortest stint of his career with any team.

As usual, it was more Rodman's lack of good judgment than good rebounding that did him in. On February 16, 2000, the NBA fined Rodman $10,000 and suspended him for one game for verbally abusing officials and failing to leave promptly after his ejection. At least Rodman didn't head-butt an official, as he did on March 18, 1996, in New Jersey, an incident that cost him $20,000 in fines. Nor, for that matter, did he make any disparaging remarks about religion, as he did about the Mormon population in 1997. Fine: $50,000.

"Me and [NBA commissioner] Dave Stern need to clear out our differences," Rodman said after he was ejected for the twenty-third time in his career and received yet another stiff fine. "Let's get into the ring. He gets naked. I get naked. Let's go in and get it on, brother."

Perhaps it would have been a different story for Rodman in Dallas if the Mavericks had been winning, just as it was in Detroit with the notorious Pistons' "Bad Boys" teams that, quite literally, flattened the opposition, and as it was again in Chicago with the more sophisticated Bulls. Two teams, five NBA championships, and no regrets for either town in which Rodman had made his mark in more ways than one.

Rodman is proud of his image: *Bad As I Want To Be* is

Chicago Bulls forward Dennis Rodman reacts to a call during the third quarter of Game 5 of the 1996 NBA finals against the Seattle SuperSonics.

the title of his autobiography which includes racy images of his relationship with "The Material Girl," Madonna. A role model for resistance, Rodman might not have started the trend of wearing tattoos in the NBA, but he certainly perfected it. Find any place on his body and you'll probably find a tattoo—or at least something that's pierced: nose, ears, even private parts. And he's a cross-dresser to boot. Everything about Rodman screams *Here I am!*

Of course, his basketball talents also speak loudly. The unpredictable Rodman has never been a true leader in his basketball career, but he has been a superb complementary player. Ask Bill Laimbeer and Isiah Thomas of the Pistons or Michael Jordan and Scottie Pippen of the Bulls.

Considering his shaky beginnings, it's hard to believe that Rodman would end up in a pro basketball lineup. If anything, he seemed destined for a police lineup. One night while working as a janitor at the Dallas-Fort Worth Airport, he shoved his broom through a store window on a dare and stole some watches. The police arrested Rodman, but released him once he told them where he hid the loot.

Dennis Rodman pauses while signing his autobiography *Bad As I Wanna Be* to strike a pose for photographers. Wearing a hot pink feather boa, a silver tank top, earrings, and silver colored hair, Rodman made his entrance on a pink Harley-Davidson to the amazement of thousands of onlookers.

Rodman was more successful at stealing rebounds. At Detroit, he fit in perfectly with the Pistons, who were building an image as basketball renegades. His basketball odyssey later took him to San Antonio, Chicago, Los Angeles, and Dallas, usually accompanied by some kind of controversy on or off the court. Rodman has always played by his own rules, showing up at practices when he wanted to, if he showed up at all. He has been, at the very least, outspoken, speaking his mind on every issue from race to religion. And his off-beat, often shocking behavior would set the NBA on its ear. Nonconformity emanated from every part of him. For most observers, it was the epitome of bad taste when Rodman showed up for a book signing wearing a sequined dress and a silver wig. One writer noted that, "Rodman is giving cross-dressers a bad name."

Rodman, however, felt that he was showing his best side. "I want to challenge people's image of what an athlete is supposed to be," he said. "I like bringing out the feminine side of Dennis Rodman."

In spite of such weird behavior, there was always the talent, the sublime talent, and the ability to reach higher than anyone to grab the ball. Without question, Rodman is one of the best rebounders in NBA history. Maybe that's because winning battles in tight situations has been part of his nature since childhood.

Rodman's fearless demeanor in his private life comes into play when he is on the court, where he is a tenacious, intelligent player under the boards—some might call him a basketball genius. Many of his teammates have.

"The stigma that Dennis carries is all that stuff that he does off the court," said former Lakers teammate Rick Fox. "But he doesn't bring dancing girls and the whole [night] club to practice. He comes to work."

NBA veteran Derek Harper feels Rodman has been largely misunderstood.

"I think if you took time and really got to know him, you'd find that he's a good person," Harper said. "Under all the bull and the games that he sometimes plays, I think he's a solid dude. He's just a little different."

Tonight Show host Jay Leno presents Chicago Bulls forward Dennis Rodman with a pair of high-heeled basketball shoes during taping of *The Tonight Show*. Rodman autographed the shoes and gave them to a woman in the audience.

NEGATIVE NEWSMAKERS LIST

History may be kind to some of these sports folks, though at times their actions have been anything but sporting. Even great athletes and administrators have their bad moments.

• **Rosie Ruiz.** In one of the greatest upsets in U.S. track and field history, Rosie Ruiz was the first woman to cross the finish line in the 1980 Boston Marathon. Her time was the third-fastest ever.

How could an unknown rise to the top so fast? By cheating: Ruiz didn't run the entire race.

In their investigation, race officials learned that Ruiz did not cross any of the midrace checkpoints. Eight days after the event, she was disqualified. She never once contested the decision.

Three years later, she spent time in a Miami jail for selling cocaine to an undercover officer.

Rosie Ruiz is the first to cross the finish line in the 1980 Boston Marathon.
This astounding unknown runner posted the third fastest time ever
in the women's competition. Problem—she did not run the entire race.
Later she was disqualified. Ruiz never contested the decision.

• **R. William Jones and Renato Righetto.** Only the most avid fans of the Olympics or basketball know of them, yet they were at the center of the worst case of sports robbery. Righetto, a Brazilian, was the head referee of the 1972 Olympic basketball final between the United States and the Soviet Union. His error was ignoring the rules at the end of the game.

Even more egregious was Jones' role in the fiasco. The secretary-general of FIBA, which governs international basketball, ordered that three seconds be placed back on the clock after the game ended in an American victory which everyone else seemed ready to accept. Jones had no grounds to do so, but Righetto yielded and Soviet star Sasha Belov scored on a lay-up at the buzzer.

The U.S. players refused their silver medals. Who could blame them?

Three seconds were added but an American victory was taken away. Soviet player Ivan Edeshko raises his arms in victory after teammate Alexander Belov scored when given a second chance in the final match of the 1972 Summer Olympic Games.

NEGATIVE NEWSMAKERS LIST

● **Don Meade and Herb Fisher.** On May 6, 1933, these jockeys staged the "fighting finish" to the Kentucky Derby. Before the advent of photo-finish cameras and video patrol judging, Meade, on Brokers Tip, and Fisher, on Head Play, staged an all-out war during America's biggest race. They pushed, hit, tugged, jostled, even whipped each other to the finish line at Churchill Downs. Brokers Tip was declared the winner by about three inches.

Afterward, Fisher jumped Meade on the way back to the jockey's room.

● **Hiouad Larbi.** One of five judges in the 1988 Olympics light middleweight boxing final between American Roy Jones and South Korean Park Si-hun, Larbi is the most notorious.

While Jones (later considered to be the best professional boxer in the world) pummeled Park for all three rounds, three of the judges apparently were watching something else. They voted for Park in a decision one French newspaper called "scandalous."

Indeed. Larbi would later testify at an IOC hearing that he and other African boxing judges received $300 from Korean organizers for "expenses." He also claimed he voted for Park because he "was certain the other four judges would score the fight for the American by a wide margin."

• **Dave Kingman.** During his sixteen years in major league baseball, Dave Kingman hit 442 home runs and drove in 1,210 runs. He also drove his teammates to distraction with an untold number of practical jokes. No one was safe from Kingman's water balloons, which he tossed on the unsuspecting. Or from his stink bombs, which he unleashed in an elevator packed with players.

However, it was nothing compared to the way he tormented the media, once dumping a bucket of water on a Chicago sports writer and sending a horrifying "gift" to a female writer covering the Oakland A's. The mean-spirited Kingman made no secret of his dislike for the policy that allowed female writers into the clubhouse. So he bought a dead rat, wrapped it in a corsage box, and sent it to Susan Fornoff of the *Sacramento Bee*.

The incident, a public relations nightmare for the A's, hastened the end of Kingman's baseball career. Despite hitting thirty-five home runs and knocking in ninety-four runs in the 1986 season, Kingman was let go by the A's. No one else in the major leagues attempted to sign him. To his everlasting regret, Kingman was denied the opportunity to reach his cherished goal of 500 home runs—a figure he could have easily attained in two more seasons.

• **Avery Brundage.** The last caretaker of amateurism in the Olympics, Brundage turned his back on the Soviet bloc's blatant circumvention of Olympic eligibility rules. In his twenty-year term as president of the International Olympic Committee, he spoke against political intervention in the Games, yet he used political clout at every turn, whether it was to bar competitors or countries from the Olympics or to lobby for specific bidding sites to host the Olympics.

Brundage's worst decision came in 1972 when, after the massacre of eleven Israelis by Arab terrorists, he ordered the Munich Games to continue.

NEGATIVE NEWSMAKERS LIST

- **Barry Bonds.** One of the best all-around baseball players of the last decade, Bonds also was one of the most obnoxious toward fans. He was at his most insulting on a tour of Japan in 1990.

  For a sellout, the Japanese thanked the participants by giving each of them a coin as a token of appreciation. Bonds, in full view of everyone in the ballpark, tossed the coin away, muttering, "Who needs this?"

  He also was one of several players who "dogged it" during the tour, rarely playing hard or making an effort to create goodwill.

San Francisco Giants left fielder Barry Bonds leaps to catch a fly ball hit by the New York Mets' Todd Zeile during the third inning of their game in San Francisco.

- **Mel Hall.** Another recalcitrant outfielder, but one hardly as skilled as Bonds, Hall was playing for the Yankees when a Milwaukee youngster, set up with a fishing line and a ball attached to the end of it, lowered a note at the start of batting practice asking players for their autograph. Hall, infuriated by the ploy, took a pair of scissors from the trainer's room and cut the boy's line. The boy and his father left dejectedly.

• **Bill Laimbeer.** During his time in the NBA, Bill Laimbeer won his share of championships. He also made his share of enemies.

As one of the most physical players on the Detroit Pistons' "Bad Boys" teams, Laimbeer gloried in—and happily promoted—his image as a ruffian center.

"I have a competitive nature," he said. "I did anything I could to win, and I came off as a mean, nasty guy."

Boston's Larry Bird, among others, will testify to that. Acting like a character from the World Wrestling Federation, Laimbeer decked the Celtics' star with a body slam during a playoff game. Bird came up throwing punches, then threw the basketball at Laimbeer. Later, Bird refused to shake hands whenever the Detroit center offered.

"I've got no use for that guy," Bird said.

Neither did opposing fans. At the halftime of one game in Atlanta, a fan pulled out a chain saw. No, he didn't use it on Laimbeer—but he did on a cardboard likeness of the Pistons' most reviled player.

If it was a Western movie, Laimbeer would have had his face plastered all over post office walls. As it was, he just left his opponents plastered all over the court as the Pistons won league championships in 1989 and 1990.

"We embraced the "Bad Boys" image," Laimbeer said. "To us, it didn't matter who got in the way."

The Detroit Pistons' Bill Laimbeer proclaiming his innocence during a game with the Orlando Magic at the Palace of Auburn Hills, Michigan.

CHEATERS AND GAMBLERS

SAY IT AIN'T SO

In the 1920s, it was no big deal for baseball players to gamble—even on the games they played. It *was* a big deal, however, when the Chicago White Sox were caught trying to "fix" the 1919 World Series.

Fast forward to the 1950s, when the City College of New York (CCNY) basketball team got caught for point-shaving, along with other college teams.

The players involved were trying to make money the easy way, by cheating. But it wasn't so easy for them at the end. They paid for it big time. Just ask Pete Rose, who may not make it to Cooperstown because of his gambling habits.

Meet the wise guys who weren't so smart after all.

As "Shoeless" Joe Jackson lay dying, he saw himself stepping up to the plate in Heaven.

"I'm going to meet the greatest ump, and he knows I'm innocent," he said.

In life, the doors of baseball's Hall of Fame had been closed to him. He was blacklisted. And yet, thirty years after the infamous "Black Sox" scandal, he still professed his innocence.

Jackson could boast of having baseball's third highest career batting average (.356), but the notorious Black Sox scandal knocked him and seven teammates out of the box.

The Black Sox. Just the mention of that name conjures up the darkest incident in baseball, perhaps in American sports history. Eight Chicago White Sox players were accused of accepting bribes to lose the 1919 World Series to the Cincinnati Reds so that gamblers—and the players themselves—would benefit financially. The underdog Reds won the Series five games to

"Shoeless Joe" Jackson is shown in action during his heyday. He was one of the key figures in the infamous "Black Sox" scandal, which rocked baseball and led to the hiring of a no-nonsense commissioner for the league.

Chicago White Sox knuckleball pitcher Ed Cicotte (above) and shortstop Charles "Swede" Risberg (opposite) were both implicated in the "Black Sox" gambling scandal.

three, and the White Sox secured their ignominious place in sports history as "The Black Sox."

Although a court failed to convict the eight after a trial in 1921, baseball commissioner Kenesaw Mountain Landis banned them for life. The tough new commissioner, hired by owners to clean up baseball, said he made the decision "regardless of the verdict of juries."

Eight players up, eight down. All struck out of baseball: Shoeless Joe Jackson, Eddie Cicotte, Oscar "Happy" Felsch, Arnold "Chick" Gandil, Fred McMullin, Charles "Swede" Risberg, George "Buck" Weaver and Claude "Lefty" Williams.

According to most accounts, Gandil was the ringleader and Risberg his right-hand man. Cicotte, one of the game's best pitchers, supposedly signed a confession in which he described Gandil as the "master of ceremonies." Gandil reportedly had a history of fixing games, a common practice then according to many historians. "[Ballplayers] all mixed with gamblers [in those days]," Gandil admitted in an interview many years after the scandal.

It was Gandil's relationship with these gamblers that planted the seed for the 1919 fix. The asking price? About $80,000 to $100,000. Gandil would take care of the players, he told bookmaker Joseph "Sport" Sullivan, just take care of the money.

Apparently Sullivan did, although it's still not clear where it came from. More than one group of gamblers was involved, the most prominent being Arnold Rothstein. Before it was over, there was turmoil aplenty between the gamblers and players—the White Sox winning one game they were supposed to lose because some of the money had been withheld, and the gamblers threatening to strong-arm players if they didn't lose.

Although Gandil made a killing, not many of his teammates did. Some received less than what they were promised, some got nothing at all. Weaver, for one, never accepted any money and played some of the best baseball of his career. A former shortstop who was moved to third when Risberg took over at short, Weaver batted .324 in the Series, scored four runs, and played perfect defense while handling twenty-seven chances in the field. His crime? He knew of the conspiracy but didn't tell authorities.

The same could be said of Jackson, who batted .375 in the Series, knocked in six runs, scored five and handled sixteen chances in the field without an error. The box score seemed to validate Jackson's plea of innocence. It listed in bold black and white all of his great numbers—except the one number that counted most of all, the $5,000 payoff money Jackson accepted from a teammate.

While not necessarily proof of their guilt, the Series box score did show Gandil and Risberg performing at levels below expectations. Gandil, a first baseman who was a lifetime .277 hitter, had batted .290 during the 1919 season. In eight World Series games against the Reds, he had a .233 batting average. Risberg had hit .256 in 1919, but only .080 in the Series. In addition, he made four errors in the eight games.

Although Gandil was generally regarded as the main villain (even though he pointed out to his dying day that he "never confessed"), it was Jackson who is remembered most in regard to the scandal. This is in large measure due to his enormous talents and the romanticized stories about him. Jackson has been immortalized in stories, some of them fictionalized, and song ("Shoeless Joe from Hannibal, Mo" from the play *Damn Yankees*). So much, in fact, has been written about "Shoeless Joe" that it's often hard to separate fact from fiction.

An illiterate son of a South Carolina mill worker, "Shoeless Joe" Jackson allegedly acquired his colorful nickname after taking off a pair of uncomfortable shoes in a semi-pro game. What is known for certain is that his talent was admired by contemporaries. The great Babe Ruth admitted to patterning his swing after Jackson, who hit as high as .408 in 1911.

The most lasting image of Jackson, though, was not on a baseball field but outside a courthouse in Chicago. The papers had been full of the scandal for some time, rocking the country and shocking fans. Jackson had been called to give testimony. When he emerged from the court house, as the story goes, a tearful young fan walked up to Jackson and said:

"Say it ain't so, Joe."

Apocryphal or not, the story has lasted all these years and the expression has become a part of the American idiom.

A ROSE BY ANY OTHER NAME ...

Hall of Famers "aren't all altar guys." —*Pete Rose*

They were two greats who played baseball with similar hell-for-leather abandon. That wasn't all that Pete Rose and Ty Cobb had in common. Both were involved in scandals that clouded their baseball careers.

The parallels end there. Although Cobb lived for several agonizing months under a shadow of suspicion that he "fixed" a game, he was eventually cleared and returned to baseball in 1927. Rose, who surpassed Cobb as the career hits leader, was suspended with the agreement that he could apply for reinstatement one year later. That was 1989. Eleven years later, Rose is still out.

"It was almost like a judge saying, 'You're not guilty of murder, but I think you killed her,'" Rose says. "Then the [judge] dies and everyone just forgets about the case. They just remember what he said, to this day, and baseball is influenced by that."

The "judge" in this case was baseball commissioner A. Bartlett Giamatti, who died a week after banning Rose from baseball.

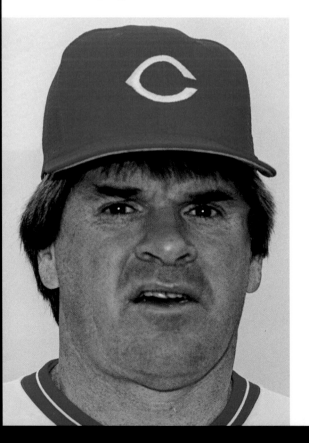

This much is known about Peter Edward Rose: an investigation by major league baseball turned up evidence that he owed hundreds of thousands of dollars in gambling debts and unpaid loans.

It was also noted that Rose hung around with unsavory characters, the type that got Brooklyn Dodgers manager Leo Durocher suspended for the 1947 season. The type that resulted in the one-year suspensions of NFL stars Paul Hornung and Alex Karras for gambling in 1963. Not to mention Denny McLain, who was banned from baseball for 132 days in 1970 for his alleged involvement in a bookmaking operation.

There was plenty of evidence against Rose that he gambled. What mainly concerned the people who ran baseball was whether Rose bet on his sport, especially when he managed the Cincinnati Reds during the 1980s.

Giamatti thought Rose bet on baseball, although he had no proof other than Rose's fingerprints on betting

Former Cincinnati Reds manager Pete Rose appears at a news conference at Riverfront Stadium on August 24, 1989, after he had been given a lifetime suspension from baseball. Since then, baseball's all-time hits leader has done jail time, hawked pizzas, done radio broadcasts, and sold his famous autograph thousands of times.

receipts, which suggested that he may have bet on games while managing the Reds. Rose disputes this. "There was one fingerprint, and I got an expert that says it may not be mine."

Rose would not be the first big baseball star to bet on baseball games. It was alleged that such greats as Cobb, Tris Speaker, and Rogers Hornsby had also gambled on a regular basis. But perhaps no more so than Hal Chase, a National League first baseman from 1905–1919, who was the busiest gambler of his time. Chase, accused by three managers of fixing games, was eventually banned from baseball.

It's more than likely, though, that Rose was a worse gambler than all of them combined. The gambling issue wasn't Rose's only black mark. He also served time in jail for tax evasion.

Cobb and Speaker were allegedly involved in a scheme to "fix" a game between their teams in 1919—ironically, the same year of the Chicago Black Sox scandal. Cobb and Speaker were, respectively, the player-managers for the Detroit Tigers and the Cleveland Indians.

The charges against Cobb and Speaker surfaced in 1926, brought forward by former Tigers pitcher Hubert "Dutch" Leonard. He said money was exchanged so that the Indians would lose to the Tigers, hopefully assuring Detroit of third place in the American League standings and a higher runners-up share from the World Series. The Indians had already clinched second place. Also allegedly involved was Cleveland outfielder Smokey Joe Wood.

The Tigers won 9-5, but it didn't help. The New York Yankees eventually finished third, half a game ahead of Detroit. And, seven years later, Cobb and Speaker were on the hot seat being grilled by iron-fisted commissioner Kenesaw Mountain Landis.

Public sentiment was on the ballplayers' side and, so it would appear, was Landis. Although American League president Ban Johnson forced Cobb and Speaker to resign their managerial positions—their teams had cut them—Landis cleared both players of the gambling charges.

Both Cobb and Speaker came back to baseball with two different teams the following season, their place assured in the Hall of Fame. Rose still awaits his turn.

After two decades as rivals, Ty Cobb and Tris Speaker finally became teammates on the Philadelphia Athletics in 1928. But two years earlier Cobb and Speaker were investigated for allegedly being involved in a scheme to "fix" a game between their teams in 1919—ironically, the same year of the Chicago "Black Sox" scandal.

SHAME OF THE GAME

In 1950, City College of New York (CCNY) pulled off the unprecedented feat of winning both the NCAA and NIT basketball championships. This amazing accomplishment is not, however, what most fans remember about the Beavers.

Once the toast of New York, the Beavers fell into disgrace when rumors began to surface that some of their players had accepted money from gamblers to "shave" points in games. Gamblers bet on point margins, not just results. A crooked player could make a lot of money by making sure that his team won by less than the expected margin. They could even lose and he would still come out a winner. All he had to do was to play poorly on purpose.

As would later be revealed, the practice of point-shaving had been going on for some time in college basketball, and to a much larger extent than anyone had envisioned. Isolated cases had been reported, most notably at Brooklyn College, but without much damage to the sport's integrity.

The tip of the iceberg surfaced at Manhattan College on January 11, 1951, when Manhattan Jaspers star Junius Kellogg was approached by Hank Poppe, a former Manhattan player fronting for the gamblers. Kellogg, still shaking from the experience, told coach Ken Norton that day he had been offered $1,000 to make sure the Jaspers lost by more than nine points to DePaul.

Kellogg, of course, had tossed Poppe out of his room. What self-respecting college athlete would take money to purposely lose, or "shave," points?

Plenty, as it turned out.

At that point, though, Norton was concerned about trapping Poppe and his gambling cohorts. Now working with authorities, Kellogg got back to Poppe and told him that he had reconsidered and would accept his offer.

Madison Square Garden was alive with excitement when DePaul came in to play Manhattan on the night of January 16. During warmups, Poppe gave Kellogg some quick instructions:

"Remember, on the rebounds miss the ball occasionally or throw hook shots over the basket. After the rebounds, don't pass as fast. That might save two points. Don't try too hard to block the other guy's shot.

"And," Poppe added meaningfully, "don't *stink* up the joint."

Kellogg was so nervous, he did. Fortunately for the Jaspers, his replacement, Charlie Genering, played better and Manhattan won 62-59. Not long after, Poppe and his gambling associates were in police custody, quickly confessing to misdeeds.

Poppe told police not only about his bribery attempts but also about some games he had fixed as a player. He and Jack Byrnes, as co-captains of the 1949–1950 Manhattan team, received weekly retainers of forty dollars each from the gamblers. For three Manhattan defeats (against Bradley, Santa Clara, and Siena), they had received $1,000 after each game. They were also paid cash for helping Manhattan win two games by scores that fit the gamblers' needs.

The arrest of Poppe and his associates was the first big break for authorities against the gamblers. For years they had pursued nothing but shadows.

"If these termites have been putting money in front of my boys' faces," said Norton, "there must be others that are falling."

Seven people are booked in Elizabeth Street Police Station, New York City, February 18, 1951, in connection with "fixed" basketball games. Left to right are Ed Warner and Al Roth, both of CCNY; Harvey (Connie) Schaff of NYU; a detective; Salvatore Tarto Sollazzo (bending down) a jewelry manufacturer; Robert Sabbatini (head down), and Ed Roman of CCNY. Eddie Gard, who played with LIU, is hidden behind Roman. Six were booked on bribery charges while Sabbatini was booked as a material witness in the case.

The district attorney's office couldn't have agreed more and, by week's end, was working on leads that went well beyond New York City. Norton didn't know it at the time, but many of his coaching colleagues were about to be rudely awakened by a national expose´. He had no idea how widespread the problem had become.

Kentucky coach Adolph Rupp, who had bragged that "gamblers couldn't touch my players with a ten-foot pole," soon had to eat his words as the widespread gambling scandal touched his school and ripped college basketball apart.

This is what authorities discovered:

Several players from CCNY played ball with gamblers. So did three stars from a Kentucky team that had won two successive NCAA championships—Alex Groza, Ralph Beard, and Dale Barnstable. Also, Long Island University's Sherman White and Bradley's Gene Melchiorre, two of the top basketball players in the country, were involved with gamblers. There were eight players alone from LIU who admitted to conspiring with gamblers.

New York University and Toledo University were brought into the expanding investigations as well. Some 700 miles apart, their geographic differential only emphasized how far the gamblers' tentacles had reached. College administrators had the word of bookies that ten million dollars was being wagered daily on college basketball games throughout the country, and there was no telling how much of this was point-shaving money.

All told, thirty-two players from seven schools were implicated in fixing eighty-seven games from 1947–1951, the lives and careers of the players damaged beyond repair. Damaged also was the reputation of Madison Square Garden, where many of the fixes occurred in New York. The Garden took a long time to recover from the scandal. College basketball in New York has never been the same.

Numerous other point-shaving scandals and fixes followed, most notably a shocker involving Jack Molinas in the early 1960s. Molinas, an NBA player who had been suspended in 1954 for gambling, was charged with operating a nationwide ring that fixed college basketball games and sentenced to between ten and fifteen years in prison. Eventually caught up in the scandal were fifty players from thirty-two schools, involving sixty-seven games. Molinas had a hand in much of the action.

Although the second scandal involved more players and schools, the scandal of 1951 was considered the granddaddy of them all because it was the first big breakthrough for authorities. And all thanks to Kellogg, whose integrity was rare in a time of trouble and greed in college basketball.

Guard Al Roth and center Ed Roman, two of the City College of New York players held on bribery charges, are shown in action in the CCNY-Missouri game at Madison Square Garden, New York, on December 9, 1950. This game is one listed by District Attorney Frank S. Hogan in an alleged "fixing" scandal. Missouri, the underdog, won 54–37.

OTHER NOTABLE SCANDALS

The 1951 and 1961 point-shaving scandals were by far the two biggest on record in American college sports history.

Here are some other notable scandals involving point-shaving and gambling:

• In 1952, Kentucky took another big hit when All-American center **Bill Spivey** was caught taking money from gamblers and barred from sports at the university.

• In 1981, former Boston College player **Rick Kuhn** and four others were found guilty of shaving points during the 1978–79 season. Kuhn was sentenced to ten years in jail.

• In 1985, **John Williams** of Tulane faced charges of scheming to fix games. Five months later, the charges were dropped.

• In 1996, Boston College suspended thirteen football players for the final three games of the 1996 season after an investigation into gambling on the team. Eventually six men were indicted in connection with a gambling ring.

• In 1998, four former Northwestern basketball players were indicted on charges of shaving points and another former athlete was indicted for other gambling incidents.

• In 1999, a federal grand jury returned an indictment against four men who conspired with Arizona State players **Stevin "Hedake" Smith** and **Isaac Burton** to fix games during the 1993–1994 season. Players and gamblers alike received sentences.

• Also in 1999, Northwestern University was all over the front pages with a gambling scandal that involved eleven football players.

Rick Kuhn was one of five people named in indictments handed down in Boston College's federal district court on charges of conspiring to fix point spreads on a number of the school's games.

Northwestern's Dion Lee (10) was indicted March 26, 1998, in Chicago on charges of shaving points in three of the school's basketball games during the 1994-95 season.

TRASH TALKERS

NASTY, SUPERBRAT, AND JIMBO

Yada. Yada. Yada. These guys all talk a good game. They also talk a *bad* game, as in trash talk.

From Nastase to McEnroe to Connors. Payton to Barkley. Yes, even Bird. During their careers, they all had something to say while beating their opponents' brains out. And it usually wasn't very nice.

They were the lips that made you flip, the wise guys who *lowered* the art of conversation.

In a word, *irreverent*.

He cursed the officials. He destroyed his racket. He made obscene gestures.

Just another day on the court for Ilie Nastase, who set the standard for bad manners in sports.

It would be hard to find an athlete who behaved more tastelessly than Nastase. Unless it was John McEnroe. Add Jimmy Connors to the mix and you truly have The Unholy Trio of Tennis.

Nastase was the first of tennis' "bad boys."

LEFT: Ilie Nastase in action at the 1976 U.S. Open against Dick Stockton. RIGHT: Nastase argues with the referee after both he and opponent Arthur Ashe were disqualified from Stockholm's $100,000 Masters Tournament. Ashe walked off the court in disgust after Nastase twice received warnings from the referee for his antics.

Then along came Connors and McEnroe to challenge the civility of their sport—and the sensibilities of our society—with their foul language and outrageous gestures.

There have been a number of other rebellious tennis players, of course, but none who quite equaled the conduct of "Nasty," "Superbrat," and "Jimbo."

During his reign of terror in the 1970s and 1980s, "Ilie the Terrible" was one of the most controversial athletes in sports. He came roaring out of Romania with his shoot-from-the-lip style and a total disdain for authority.

None of this would have meant very much had Nastase been just another player on the tour. But because he was so good—he was ranked No. 1 in the world in 1973—he drew attention wherever he went.

"This is a great player," Arthur Ashe once said of Nastase. "When he tightens up his court manners, he'll be even better."

Also known as The Bucharest Buffoon, Nastase was known for such antics as dropping his pants during a match, whacking a photographer with a towel, and playing tennis with an umbrella. Once, at the French Open, he and fellow bad-boy Connors entered the match on crutches just for the fun of it.

One of Nastase's most outrageous outbursts occurred at the U.S. Open in 1976 during a match with Germany's Hans-Juergen Pohmann. He swore at spectators, swung a racket at an umpire, and cursed and spat at Pohmann as the crowd booed lustily. Nastase's wife, Dominique, was so embarrassed that she rushed out of the stadium in tears.

Nastase quite naturally drew a fine for this display of poor sportsmanship, adding to his growing reputation as a sports villain. But he had nothing on Connors—and nothing on McEnroe, who seemingly used Nastase as his role model.

Connors and McEnroe began one of the most storied—and one of the most vitriolic—rivalries in sports when they met in the semifinals at Wimbledon in the early 1970s. The pair dominated men's tennis for the better part of eleven years, from July 29, 1974, until September 8, 1985. During that time, they combined to hold

Tennis star John McEnroe argues a call made by umpire Jerry Armstrong during his match against Michael Chang. McEnroe was in his old form, combining terrific tennis with his own sense of decorum.

the top spot in the ATP rankings for 438 of 580 weeks. They won fifteen grand slam tournaments between them, including nine U.S. Open and five Wimbledon titles.

Observers likened a Connors-McEnroe match to a titanic fight between two great heavyweights. No love was lost between these two, and they were always going for the knockout punch.

Once, at Wimbledon, Connors told McEnroe that his two-year-old son was more mature. "You're a phony!" McEnroe shot back.

When they weren't feuding with each other, they were feuding with the establishment. At the 1984 Davis Cup, McEnroe and Connors behaved

Jimmy Connors reaches for the ball during the Wimbledon Men's Singles Championship Final against John McEnroe.

so badly that the United States Tennis Association issued a code of conduct guideline for future tournaments. The guideline stressed that U.S. Davis Cup players should "act with courtesy and civility toward competitors, officials, and spectators."

Following world-class tantrums by McEnroe and Connors at the Davis Cup, USTA Davis Cup chairman Gordon Jorgenson stressed that "abusive language . . . gestures . . . abuse of rackets, balls and courtside accessories—all such irresponsible behavior should not be tolerated."

Connors said he "resented getting a carbon copy in the mail" regarding the code of conduct guidelines. "I consider myself and [John] McEnroe big enough boys that [USTA officials] could come in and talk to us face-to-face."

Connors, an Illinois native, had studied under Pancho Segura on the West Coast and joined Bill Riordan's tennis troupe before joining the pros.

He was angry, abrasive and irreverent, an anti-establishment rebel known for such colorful habits as grinding his groin and jabbing his finger—what one writer described as a "punk-rock act."

Connors retired the "Biggest Jerk in Sports" trophy with one outrageous display late in his career. Connors was playing Ivan Lendl in an exhibition match for charity in Kissimmee, Florida, on March 24, 1985. The linesperson was Jan Enos, a sixty-seven-year-old grandmother with a solid background in tennis. Enos, who was donating her time that day to work the lines, listed the 1976 U.S. Open on her resume.

When one of her calls went against Connors, he showed his displeasure by holding his nose and playfully wagging a finger at Enos. When another call went against him, he hit a ball hard in her direction, missing Enos by a couple of feet. The third call against Connors sent him out of control. He again fired the ball at Enos, this time missing her head by inches.

Enos could take no more. She picked up her things and walked out. "Twice he tried to hit me," she said. "I had to get out or I'd have two belly buttons. I was surprised at him. This was an exhibition, not Wimbledon."

McEnroe was no less volatile on the court. If anything, his behavior was even worse than Connors'; McEnroe had a devil of a time controlling himself. "I'd think, 'You're going out to play, and you're not gonna yell at the umpire,'" McEnroe said. "And within two games I'd be pissed off and yell at the umpire. It was an alter-ego thing, like Jekyll and Hyde. My bad part overpowered me."

And when he was bad, he was very, very bad. In 1985 he alienated just about everyone on the U.S. Davis Cup team—including the mild-mannered Ashe, who was captain—and was suspended.

It was at staid, old Wimbledon that McEnroe had some of his biggest blow-ups. Many of the English will never forgive him; they certainly won't forget him—not when he called one of their own "the pits of the world."

These choice words were directed at a Wimbledon umpire in 1981, who also heard this from McEnroe: "I am not having points taken off me by an incompetent old fool." Another McEnroe gem: "You must arrest him! He is the worst umpire I have ever seen."

Nor did McEnroe mellow after leaving tennis, making occasionally acerbic TV appearances as a broadcaster. Even driving a car to and from work, McEnroe was back to his old tricks. Talk about road rage!

"By the time I drive home," he says, "Fifty people have called me an a———."

Then they get a glimpse behind the wheel.

"Sometimes a guy will yell, 'Hey, that a———'s John McEnroe. Now I know why he's driving like that.'"

McEnroe's spectacular play and volatile on-court behavior attracted fans to the game of tennis.

John McEnroe kicks a television camera he felt was crowding him on the court during the finals of the U.S. Pro Indoor Tennis Championships in Philadelphia.

THE MOUTHS THAT ROAR

Reggie Miller is a handful for anyone guarding him on a basketball court. He's also one of the leading trash-talkers in the NBA. After all these years, the loquacious Indiana Pacers guard hasn't mellowed one bit.

"I'll still talk mess," he says, "I just won't talk it to the referees."

For Miller, as it is for many athletes in sports, trash-talking is an invaluable part of his game. Miller claims it gives him a psychological edge over his opponent.

"That's how basketball has always been played," Miller says. "You can't take the street out of basketball. You can't expect us to be robots out there. You have to let us show emotion. If we didn't, it'd be like golf." In a poll conducted by a national sports magazine a couple of years ago, Miller was listed in a "top five" of the NBA's leading trash-talkers. Seattle's Gary Payton was No. 1, followed by Michael Jordan, Charles Barkley, Miller and Tim Hardaway.

"I say everything," Payton said. "I mean, I use everything. You always talk about somebody, especially if he got me with a move or something. You try to tease them all the time."

Payton's favorite line when playing shorter players like Muggsy Bogues: "There's a mouse in the house."

Once an opponent dared Payton to shoot. He did—and hit a three-pointer. "That's why I make twelve million," he said, walking past his challenger.

The recently retired Barkley says trash-talk has always been a part of the NBA. But the tenor of the talk changed in the '90s.

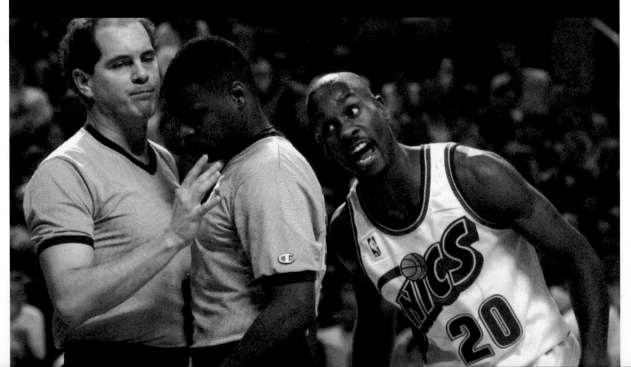

In a poll conducted by a national sports magazine, Seattle's Gary Payton was listed as the No. 1 trash-talker in the NBA. Payton's favorite line when playing shorter players is "There's a mouse in the house."

"In the good old days," Barkley said, "you just talked to have fun. Now there's a vindictiveness in your voice. I think it's in the players' mentality. They make so much money, they've got long-term guaranteed contracts, and they turn into jerks."

Some of Barkley's talk was translated into the written word. When he played for the Philadelphia 76ers, Barkley once wrote an obscene note to Detroit center Bill Laimbeer and had it delivered by a locker-room attendant before a game. It came as no surprise when a brawl broke out during the game and Barkley and Laimbeer were in the middle of it.

"Charles Barkley is not [Sir] Charles with his mouth shut on the court," Jordan once said. "That's like me playing with hair."

Jordan should talk. Before he retired, "Air Jordan" might have been described as "Hot Air" Jordan.

Charles Barkley took trash-talk one step forward by writing an obscene note to Detroit center Bill Laimbeer and having it delivered before the game.

"Michael would be out there telling you, 'I'm driving to the basket, and there's nothing you can do,'" said B.J. Armstrong, who played with Jordan in Chicago.

Even Jordan's own teammates felt his fury. Armstrong said that Jordan's belittling remarks in practice hurt his confidence. Quite often, Jordan didn't have to say anything to intimidate.

"He just gave you a stare," said Portland guard Steve Smith. "It was more of a trash *look*."

Larry Bird, meanwhile, was another one to back up his words with action.

"Bird would tell guys what he-was getting ready to do and ask them if they were ready," remembered Brian Shaw, a former teammate of Bird's. "I le would say, 'Okay, I'm going to make this one off the backboard; are you ready?' Then, he would shoot it off the backboard and make it and say, 'Oh, I thought you said you were ready.'"

Typical Bird by-play: In the middle of a game, he would walk over to the opposing team's bench and ask the coach: "Can you put somebody in that can check me? He [the player guarding Bird] can't check me."

Basketball doesn't have a monopoly on trash-talking. Football and hockey, because of the constant face-to-face contact, also feature their fair share. And it's not always in good fun. Because of recent racial slurs by players during games, the NHL has issued a "zero tolerance" policy in such cases. And, of course, Atlanta Braves pitcher John Rocker rocked the baseball establishment with trash-talking of another kind when he condemned just about everyone in a national magazine story after the Braves' loss to the New York Yankees in the 1999 World Series.

In football, there's the Minnesota Vikings' John Randle, a dedicated student of trash-talk. Randle actually studies team media guides, pre-game press notes, and newspapers for personal information that he might use to turn against his opponents.

The best trash-talker of all time? Muhammad Ali deserves consideration. No one was better at humbling an opponent with words than the former heavyweight boxing champion.

Try this: "You think the world was shocked when Nixon resigned? Wait till I whup George Foreman's behind."

Which he promptly did.

On "Bloody Sunday," in a game between the San Francisco Giants and the Los Angeles Dodgers, Giants' pitcher Juan Marichal swings his bat and hits catcher John Roseboro twice in the head. Marichal was fined $1,750 (a record for the time), suspended for eight games, and barred from attending a series in LA for fear of starting a riot.

VILLAINOUS HEROES

Even some of the best athletes, people who have made Halls of Fame, won MVP honors and all sorts of championship titles, have resorted to trickery. Maybe they have behaved poorly, saying or doing the least sportsmanlike thing in a very public setting.

Do they qualify as villains? Not necessarily. They could be heroes such as Dale Earnhardt, known as The Intimidator for good reason. As good a race car driver as anyone who ever sat behind the wheel, he also would do—and has done—anything to get to the checkered flag first.

It could be a superb pitcher such as Juan Marichal temporarily losing his sanity and clubbing an opponent on the head with a bat. Or a Masters champion like Fuzzy Zoeller unwisely opening his mouth wide enough to shove his entire golf bag into it.

Witness the villainous heroes—or the heroic villains, depending on your point of view.

JUAN MARICHAL

Marichal, possibly the top Latin American pitcher ever, needed three tries to get into the Hall of Fame, and he knows why.

It was because of what he did on August 22, 1965, when Marichal's San Francisco Giants met their archrivals, the Los Angeles Dodgers.

"The first year I didn't make the Hall of Fame," he said after he was voted into the Cooperstown shrine in 1983, "I looked at the records of the pitchers who were in there. At that time, there were forty-two. My record was better than thirty-two of them."

But none of them had clubbed an opposing catcher over the head with a bat.

On what became known as "Bloody Sunday," Marichal was at bat against Sandy Koufax in a matchup of the teams' best pitchers. The pennant race was hot, and Marichal got even hotter while at bat in the third inning. On the second pitch, Roseboro returned the ball to Koufax by throwing it just past Marichal's ear.

Marichal claimed Roseboro then came out of his crouch, his fist clenched. Roseboro later admitted that he was retaliating for Giants pitchers throwing at Dodgers batters during the series, because he knew Koufax would not reciprocate for fear of killing someone with his 100 mph fastball.

"He didn't say anything, just came at me," Marichal said. "I thought he would hit me with his mask, so I hit him."

Marichal took his bat and brought it down twice on Roseboro's head. With blood streaming down the catcher's face, both benches emptied.

Willie Mays, among the greatest and most respected of all ballplayers and a close friend of Roseboro's, calmed things by immediately examining Roseboro's wound and talking to him.

Marichal was ejected and Roseboro was removed from the game, though he was not hurt seriously. National League president Warren Giles fined Marichal $1,750, a record at the time, and suspended him for eight games. Marichal was also barred from attending a September series in Los Angeles for fear of starting a riot.

Roseboro filed a $110,000 damage suit against Marichal that was settled out of court for $7,500 in 1970. But after years of bitterness, Marichal and Roseboro became friends, playing golf together or appearing at old timers' games.

"The first year I didn't make the Hall of Fame I looked at the records of the pitchers who were there. At that time, there were forty-two. My record was better than thirty-two of them," said pitcher Juan Marichal after he was finally voted into Cooperstown.

HEADHUNTERS AND SPIT-BALLERS

They threw at heads or doctored baseballs. Either way, the pitchers who intentionally hit batters or used illegal pitches violated the spirit of the game.

Yet it's impossible to ignore the records of a Bob Gibson or Don Drysdale, both in the Hall of Fame, or a Sal Maglie, known as "The Barber" for the close shaves he gave hitters.

And it's unfair to label Gaylord Perry nothing more than a cheater because, well, he did get away with throwing a spitball (or some variation thereof) for twenty-two years and won 314 games on his way to Cooperstown.

Back in the early days of the major leagues, the spitball was legal. Such pitchers as Burleigh Grimes and Stan Coveleski built Hall of Fame

careers using it, and were allowed to continue throwing wet ones even after the spitball was outlawed in 1921.

Perry never had such permission. He was never caught, disavowing use of the illegal pitch until he wrote a book in 1974, his thirteenth major league season.

A relief pitcher who seemed destined for a mediocre career with the San Francisco Giants, Perry came under the tutelage of veteran Bob Shaw. What Shaw taught Perry was simple: how to doctor the ball without anyone figuring out how it was done.

While Perry didn't throw a spitball on every pitch, batters thought he did. His gestures on the mound convinced batters that, when Perry either touched his sideburns or the bill of his cap or his uniform, he was loading up—a huge psychological edge for the pitcher.

In his first season as a spitballer, Perry went from 1-6 with a 4.03 ERA to 12-11 with a 2.75 ERA.

From there, he became one of the more consistent winners for seven teams and a recipient of the Cy Young Award in both the American League (1972) and National League (1978).

So why did he turn to the spitball?

"I thought of my wife Blanche, our very young children, and Mama and Daddy back home on the farm, all counting on me," he wrote. "I figured if I could master that super pitch, I'd be buying time to develop some other pitches . . . The old dewdrop takes total dedication, like any new pitch you learn, only more so."

Wetting the ball was not an option for Gibson, Drysdale, or Maglie. Nor was allowing a batter to crowd the plate.

While Gibson won 257 games and entered the Hall of Fame in 1981, and Drysdale won

Bob Gibson made sure he owned the plate by pitching batters inside.

209 and was enshrined in 1984, both were known as much for their brushback as for their otherwise impressive stats.

Drysdale hit 154 batters and led the National League in that category five times.

"I had one rule I stuck to," Drysdale once said. "Nobody was going to crowd the plate on me. If someone did and I hit him, and he kept crowding, he knew he might get hit again . . . and again."

Gibson was also known to throw at batters: behind them, in front of them—anywhere he could to make a statement.

"If a hitter thought he could get close [to home plate] and reach that outside pitch and punch it the other way, I had to show him he couldn't do that," Gibson said. "I had to make sure he knew he couldn't do that."

So he pitched them inside.

But nobody was better at the close shave than Maglie, who got his nickname of "The Barber" for doing precisely that. Maglie had such an awesome curveball that he could make it break just before it came in on a batter.

But he wasn't shy about making contact, either.

"I'm out there playing catch with my catcher," he once said. "That guy with the bat is just in the way. If he isn't doing just what I want, then I had to teach him where to stand and what to do."

Does he or doesn't he? Gaylord Perry was notorious for throwing spitballs, though he was never caught. Often his gestures on the mound had batters convinced a spitball was coming, which definitely gave Perry the psychological advantage.

"She's here with her girlfriend. She's half a man," said Martina Hingis of Amelie Mauresmo, her opponent in the 1999 Austrailian Open final.

MARTINA HINGIS

By the time she was sixteen, the Swiss miss with the stinging groundstrokes was the top-ranked tennis player in the world. She also became the youngest Wimbledon champion in 1997.

Hingis wasn't nearly as smooth with her words as she was moving around the court. At the 1999 Australian Open, she was asked about her opponent in the final, France's Amelie Mauresmo.

"She's here with her girlfriend. She's half a man," Hingis reportedly said in German, remarks Hingis then denied, claiming she had "nothing to apologize for."

But Mauresmo, who spoke publicly about being a lesbian, noted that the interview with Hingis was on tape for all the world to hear. When the match ended in a 6-2, 6-3 win for Hingis, Mauresmo icily shook hands at the net, then skipped the traditional peck on each cheek.

Lindsay Davenport had made a remark about Mauresmo's muscularity during the tournament, and when that was misconstrued, Davenport apologized both publicly and privately. Hingis did not.

"I'd like to make a distinction between Davenport, who not only apologized but also wrote a personal note to Amelie, and Hingis' behavior, which was disappointing," said Christophe Fournerie, Mauresmo's coach. "And I can tell you that Amelie told her that on the court today."

DIEGO MARADONA

Argentina's soccer wizard, who led his nation to the 1986 World Cup title and into the championship game four years later, remains an icon at home, though it certainly hasn't been for his behavior off the field.

The creativity and combativeness Maradona displayed in games made it impossible to take your eyes off him. But his battles with teams, the media, and drugs have been painful to watch.

Maradona was twice banned from international competition after testing positive for drugs, including during the 1994 World Cup. A positive test for cocaine in 1991 prompted a fifteen-month suspension from the Italian League, where he played for Napoli. During the World Cup three years later, a "cocaine cocktail" he took got him kicked out of the tournament and banned for another fifteen months. Maradona's cocaine use eventually led to serious heart disease.

He was also involved in several contract disputes, routinely walking out on agreements with one team to join another. And he received a two-year suspended sentence for a February 1994 incident when he fired an air rifle at photographers and journalists outside his country home.

Diego Maradona, a creative and talented player who led Argentina to the 1986 World Cup title, had a history of drug abuse that eventually led to serious heart disease.

Fuzzy Zoeller's remarks about Tiger Woods led to a cancellation of his contract with his main sponsor, Kmart. "We have to stop being so sensitive about things," Zoeller said about another incident involving yet another black player.

FUZZY ZOELLER

Zoeller, the 1979 Masters and 1984 U.S. Open champion, is a fun-loving guy who enjoys bantering with his playing partners, caddies, and fans during tournaments. He's one of the more jovial, relaxed, and colorful players on the tour.

In 1997, however, he became a bit too colorful.

During a golf outing shortly after Tiger Woods had won the '97 Masters, Zoeller called Woods "that little boy" and suggested he not put fried chicken or collard greens on the menu for the champions dinner at Augusta.

Zoeller claimed to be joking, but his main sponsor, Kmart, canceled his contract immediately.

During the 1998 Thornblade Classic in Greenville, South Carolina, Zoeller had this exchange with his friend Victor McBryde, who is black.

"Hey, Fuzzy," McBryde yelled from the tee box two holes ahead of Zoeller. Zoeller shouted to McBryde to "get you some fried chicken."

McBryde told Zoeller not to forget the "cornbread." And Zoeller replied, "How about some watermelon?"

Zoeller wondered why such a conversation made news.

"We have to stop being so sensitive about things," Zoeller said. "I'm white, Vic McBryde is black, so what? I kidded him, he kidded me back. If we don't all learn to laugh at each other and ourselves, we're not ever going to get along."

Conrad Dobler (left) of the St. Louis Cardinals tries to block a charging George Martin of the New York Giants. Dobler received a 15-yard penalty for "illegal use of hands" in trying to protect his quarterback.

CONRAD DOBLER

Getting along was not part of the job description for Dobler. A solid if not outstanding offensive tackle for ten seasons, Dobler earned a reputation for nastiness with his mouth—not by talking but by biting.

"But it was like everything else I did," Dobler said about his munching on opponents. "It was victim-precipitated violence. I was aggressive. I didn't think I was dirty."

During a 1974 playoff game, Minnesota Vikings defensive lineman Doug Sutherland was the victim.

"He kept sticking his fingers through my facemask," Dobler said. "I figured he was not there to stroke my mustache. It was not a friendly act. So I bit him."

Sutherland was so bitten up by halftime that he asked Vikings officials for baseball shinguards to protect the area Dobler seemed most fond of. Oh yes, he also asked to be tested for rabies.

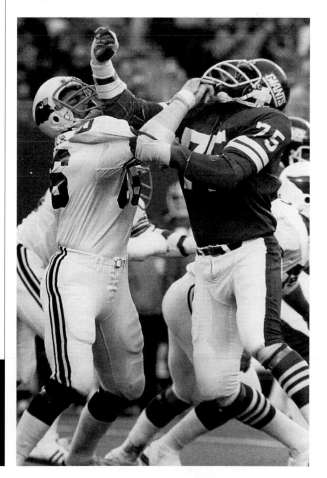

ERIC LINDROS

A franchise player. That's what Lindros was supposed to be. Another Wayne Gretzky or Mario Lemieux.

Instead, for most of his disappointing career, he has been a petulant, often puerile prima donna. A dangerous scorer and checker when he is healthy (which hasn't been often enough to suit the Philadelphia Flyers), for sure. He can even be a dominant player on some nights.

Still, Lindros generally has not lived up to expectations on the ice. And even before he made it to the NHL, he turned off not only a city (Quebec) but the French-Canadian community as a whole.

Picked first in the 1991 draft by Quebec, he refused to sign with the Nordiques and sat out an entire NHL season, playing instead for the Canadian national team. He made disparaging remarks about Nordiques owners Marcel Aubut and belittled the city, saying it was not "big league."

"I think there is a lot of overreaction," Lindros said. "It's just a case of one particular player didn't want to play for one particular owner."

Well, not exactly. Politics was also involved. Lindros eventually made it clear that he felt uncomfortable in a city dominated by a culture different from the rest of English-speaking Canada. And as a native of Ontario province, he was strongly against the French separatist movement to make Quebec province an independent country. Lindros stood by the comments of his father and agent, who said no amount of money could get Eric to play in Quebec.

"We're absolutely solid in the position that Eric will not play hockey for the Nordiques," Carl Lindros said. "It doesn't make sense for Eric. And if somebody was to really pull back and look at it, I'm not sure it makes sense for the Nordiques.

"And once he expresses his views, that Quebec should be an integral part of Canada . . .

then all of a sudden his position in the community—just as his going through a series of situations right now where he's uncomfortable about his personal well-being—it could get to that extreme again."

For his first game in Quebec after being acquired by the Flyers, a local radio station urged fans to show up with baby pacifiers and bibs to razz Lindros for "his spoiled brat

approach" to the Nordiques.

Lindros did force a trade to Philadelphia in 1992, and the Nordiques moved to Colorado in 1995. And while he became an on-again, off-again star with the Flyers, one of the six people for whom he was traded, Peter Forsberg, became a champion with Colorado and one of the NHL's best players. And a draft pick acquired in the deal eventually netted the Avalanche goalie Patrick Roy, another star of the Av's ascension.

Meanwhile, Lindros became involved in an ugly feud with Flyers general manager Bob Clarke in 2000 about how the team's medical staff handled his concussions. Lindros criticized the Flyers, who in turn stripped the sidelined star of his captaincy.

Certainly there were people in Quebec who were smiling about that.

Using a strategy that continued to push his competitor to the outside rail, jockey Angel Cordero rode his mount to win the Preakness in 1980. His technique so angered bettors and spectators that he was forced to hire a bodyguard. "... now in the '90's, when I watch horse racing, I see horses doing the same thing," said Cordero.

ANGEL CORDERO

There were many memorable races among the 7,075 he won. Cordero took the Kentucky Derby three times (1974 aboard Cannonade, 1976 with Bold Forbes, 1985 on Spend A Buck), the Preakness twice and the Belmont once.

He was inducted into the Hall of Fame in 1988, and when he retired four years later, he was third on the career victories list behind Bill Shoemaker and Laffit Pincay Jr., and second in lifetime purses.

Cordero was also a fine ambassador for the sport—except to fans of Genuine Risk.

In 1980, Genuine Risk became the first filly in sixty-five years to win the Kentucky Derby. America took the horse to heart, and she was a strong favorite heading into the Preakness, the second race of the Triple Crown.

When the horses entered the stretch run at Pimlico, Cordero took his mount, Codex, and moved him to the outside. As Genuine Risk came roaring up to challenge, Cordero kept moving his horse out, nudging the filly toward the outside rail. He kept on nudging and nudging until Genuine Risk ran out of steam and faded. Codex won by four and three-quarters lengths.

Cordero so angered bettors and spectators that a bomb squad was called in to check his car. For more than a year, Cordero received angry letters, many from women. He was even forced to hire a bodyguard after receiving death threats.

"Every kind of letter that came after that was bad. They got very personal," Cordero said. "They called me a disgrace and told me to go home to Puerto Rico. It was something that I didn't enjoy.

"There was a lot of controversy over that race, and now, in the '90s, when I watch racing, I see a lot of horses doing the same thing," Cordero said. "It's very normal now. At the time, there was a real bad spirit for me. It was one of the worst nightmares of my life that I won the Preakness and didn't get to enjoy it until years later."

Still, he kept on racing and, generally, having fun at it.

"I loved the public, even when they booed me," he said. "As long as they came and bet, I never cared if they booed."

DALE EARNHARDT

The two most successful drivers of the modern stock car era have been Richard Petty and Dale Earnhardt. While Petty was revered as "The King," Earnhardt has been feared, often despised by other drivers for his intimidating, get-out-of-my-way manner.

That aggressiveness has made Earnhardt as popular with the fans as any NASCAR driver. When his black No. 3 Chevy takes the lead, the folks in the grandstands from Daytona to Darlington to Dover often take to their feet cheering.

"Love him or hate, people like it when Earnhardt's near the front," said Darlington president Jim Hunter.

His fellow Winston Cup competitors aren't so

The Intimidator, Dale Earnhardt, is both loved and hated by fans—sometimes at the same time. "I just try to rattle them a little bit," Earnhardt said of his competitors. "That's just racin'."

enamored of Earnhardt. He has had running feuds with Ricky Rudd and Darrell Waltrip, and most recently his run-ins with Terry Labonte reinforced his image. And a 1999 bumping incident with Labonte actually brought Earnhardt boos, not cheers.

After Labonte passed Earnhardt for the lead with one lap to go at Bristol, Earnhardt had no room to pass back on the narrow track. So he went through Labonte, tapping him, spinning him out and heading home for the checkered flag. Labonte wound up eighth.

"You saw what happened," a livid Labonte said. "That's no way to win a race."

It was to The Intimidator.

"It was a good race between Terry and I through the race," said Earnhardt, who never saw reason to apologize for the manner in which he won. "To come to what it did and him not finish second was the only thing I hated about the whole deal and I thought back about. I wish he hadn't wrecked. I wish it would have been a deal where

we bumped and I got by him and raced on."

NASCAR saw no reason to penalize Earnhardt, despite the public and media outcry that Earnhardt intentionally wrecked another racer to win.

"We're convinced that drivers want to be able to race door-to-door and fender-to-fender without being afraid of being penalized," NASCAR CEO Mike Helton said. "Fans pay to see good, close racing. That doesn't mean we're going to let races turn into a demolition derby. That is where judgment calls have to come in.

"Drivers want to be able to race close and hard, especially on the white-flag lap. That's what we feel happened at Bristol."

What also happened at Bristol was only a temporary setback to Earnhardt's popular standing. When The Intimidator came storming down the stretch to win at Talladega two months later, there was no booing, only adulation.

"I just try to rattle them a little bit," Earnhardt said with a sly grin. "That's just racin'."

In the 1999 Goody's 500 in Bristol, Tennessee, Earnhardt (3) bumped Labonte on the final lap, causing him to wreck. Earnhardt won and Labonte finished eighth. The public and the media claimed that Earnhardt intentionally wrecked another racer to win, but NASCAR saw no reason to penalize Earnhardt.

AFTERWORD

Just because sport has been called "the sandbox of life" doesn't mean it won't include a few unruly playmates. Bearing that in mind, we have presented a good number of them in the pages of *Villains*. Perhaps we missed some of the ones you love to hate, but, alas, time and space prevented us from including everyone.

Villainy in sport is not a recent trend: that's what the gladiators were all about. Still, who can deny the element of theater present, the fascination one experiences as we watch an athlete or coach break the rules? How else, then, does one account for the popularity of wrestling?

Not that we're knocking sports villains. They often add color and spice to games that might otherwise lose our interest. After all, it's important to remember that, without villains, there would be no "good guys" to cheer.

ACKNOWLEDGMENTS

The authors wish to acknowledge the help of the following people in the research and writing of this book: Jim Litke, Richard Rosenblatt, Dave Goldberg, Hal Bock, Tim Dahlberg, Nancy Armour, Paul Newberry, Bert Rosenthal, Ben Walker, Bob Condron, Frank Carroll, Karen Rosen, JoAnn Barnas, Christine Brennan, Tom Weir, Tom Pedulla, Jim Corbett, Filip Bondy, Dave Anderson, Jere Longman, Brian Cazeneuve, Heather Linhart, Richard Oliver, John Kreiser, Aaron Heifetz, Mike Nadel, John Clayton, John Griffin, David Cooper, William Wagner, Scott Plagenhoef, Alex Gordon, Kevin Roberts, Bill Shannon, Bernie Beglane, Joel Blumberg, Steve Cohen, Lou Pintek, Mike Harris, Roy MacGregor, Mike Farrell, Steve Dryden, Mark Didtler and Lou Friedman.

ABOUT THE AUTHORS

KEN RAPPOPORT covered every major sport during his thirty-year career as a writer for The Associated Press. An award-winning freelance writer, Ken has written over twenty-five books for both adults and young readers, including biographies of Nolan Ryan, Grant Hill, Shaquille O'Neal and Wayne Gretzky.

BARRY WILNER has been a sportswriter for The Associated Press since 1976. He has covered some of the world's largest sporting events, including fifteen Superbowls, six Stanley Cups, four World Cups, and seven Olympic Games.

Rappoport and Wilner's two previous books, *They Changed the Game*, a chronicle of sports pioneers in the 20th century, and *Girls Rule!,* a look at the critical events and people that shaped women's athletics, are both published by Andrews McMeel Publishing.